About the Author

TV doctor and writer Dr David Delvin has been adviser to numerous TV programmes including BBC TV's popular *Pebble Mill at One* and ITV's *About Anglia*. A well-known 'agony uncle', he is also the author of numerous books, one of which won the Best Book Award of the American Medical Writers' Association. His medical appointments have included Medical Consultant to the Family Planning Association and he is currently a member of the General Medical Council. Dr Delvin has also been Consultant Editor on *General Practitioner* and – much to his own surprise – was awarded the Médaille de la Ville de Paris by Jacques Chirac for promoting understanding between the British and French medical professions. He is married and has three children.

AN A–Z OF
YOUR CHILD'S
HEALTH

*An Illustrated Guide to Everything a Parent
Needs to Know About Childhood Illnesses*

Dr David Delvin

CENTURY
LONDON MELBOURNE AUCKLAND JOHANNESBURG

First published in 1987 by Century Hutchinson Ltd,
Brookmount House, 62–65 Chandos Place, Covent Garden,
London WC2N 4NW

Century Hutchinson Australia Pty Ltd,
PO Box 496, 16–22 Church Street, Hawthorn, Victoria 3122,
Australia

Century Hutchinson New Zealand Ltd,
PO Box 40-086, Glenfield, Auckland 10,
New Zealand

Century Hutchinson South Africa Pty Ltd,
PO Box 337, Bergvlei, 2012 South Africa

Set in Linotron Palatino by
Rowland Phototypesetting Ltd,
Bury St Edmunds, Suffolk
Printed in Great Britain by
Scotprint, Musselburgh, Scotland

British Library Cataloguing in Publication Data
Delvin, David
An A–Z of your child's health : an illustrated
guide to everything a parent needs to know
about childhood illnesses.
1. Children—Diseases—Dictionaries
I. Title
618.92'000240431   RJ61

ISBN 0 7126 9579 6 (paper)

My thanks to:

Peter Gardiner – one of the finest medical illustrators in Britain

Valerie Woods – for deciphering my appalling writing and typing the manuscript

The various 'self-help' patient groups who've kindly assisted me with information

The practitioners of various forms of alternative medicine who've done the same

My long-suffering children

LIST OF ENTRIES

Abdominal pain
Abrasions
Abscesses
Accidents
Acne
Acupuncture
Adenoids
Air sickness
Allergies
Alopecia
Alternative medicine
Anaemia
Appendicitis
Arthritis
Aspirin
Asthma
Athlete's foot
Autism
Backache
Bad breath
Bat ears
Bed-wetting
Bee stings
Belching
Biliousness
Birthmarks
Bites
Blackheads
Bladder problems
Bleeding
Boils
Bowels
Bow legs
Breath-holding attacks
Bronchiectasis
Bronchiolitis
Bronchitis
Brucellosis
Bruises
Burns

Cancer
Car sickness
Carbon monoxide poisoning
Catarrh
Cerebral palsy
Chest disorders
Chickenpox
Chills
Chiropractic
Cholera
Chorea
Circumcision
Cleft palate and hare lip
Clinical ecology
Coeliac disease
Colds
Colic
Colitis
Colour blindness
Coma
Complementary medicine
Concussion
Congenital dislocation of the hip
Conjunctivitis
Constipation
Convulsions
Cough
Crohn's disease
Croup
Cuts
Cystic fibrosis
Cystitis
Dandruff
Deafness
Depression
Dermatitis
Diabetes
Diarrhoea
Dislocations
Dizziness

Preface

Rearing children certainly isn't easy!

I do hope that this book will help you in coping with the various symptoms and disorders which your youngster will inevitably develop during childhood. It's based on my own experiences as a doctor – and on the painful lessons learned from bringing up three children!

You'll find the book arranged in A–Z form. In an *emergency*, turn to the **First Aid** section in the middle of the book between pages 67 and 72.

One slightly unusual feature is that this medical book does actually acknowledge the existence of alternative (or complementary) medicine. At the end of the entries on many of the more important childhood conditions, you'll find a brief explanation of the way in which alternative practitioners believe that the disorder should be treated. There are also separate short entries covering the major and increasingly popular varieties of complementary medicine, such as osteopathy, chiropractic and acupuncture.

That doesn't mean that I've wasted time covering the loonier cults of the medical 'fringe'. But because large numbers of parents are becoming rather doubtful about letting orthodox doctors use powerful (and sometimes unnecessary) drugs to treat their children, I think it's only reasonable to give you a brief account of the sensible alternative treatments.

Finally, I'd like to acknowledge my debt to the late Sir Wilfrid Sheldon, who was my first 'chief' and (perhaps a bit more importantly) consultant paediatrician to HM the Queen. He taught generations of doctors that the most important things in dealing with a sick child are not drugs – but kindness and common sense.

Dr David Delvin

PS: Your children (as you'll have noticed) are either male or female. So I've used 'he' and 'she' fairly indiscriminately throughout this book: there should be about 50 per cent of each.

ABDOMINAL PAIN (*Tummy ache*)

Tummy ache in children is extremely common. But the first thing for any parent to get clear about it is that usually it isn't serious. In fact, 999 times out of 1000, a child's tummy ache will go away by itself and cause no major problems. Every now and again, a child develops abdominal pain because of some *serious* cause, such as appendicitis. But most cases of childhood tummy pain do get better very quickly.

Diagnosing abdominal pain is very difficult. So it would be ridiculous for me to try to give you any guide here as to how to make such a diagnosis. Even doctors find this very tricky. I have to admit that, for example, a high proportion of children who are sent to hospital for abdominal pain come in with a mistaken diagnosis.

However, what IS important is to have some rough idea of when a tummy ache is sufficiently bad to make it necessary to inform the doctor. In general, if a pain has been going on for less than two or three hours, it's not likely to be anything very serious. Most major causes of abdominal pain produce distress for many hours on end.

You should however be suspicious of any abdominal pain which is associated with a temperature of over 37·8°C (100°F).

Also, in a baby or young toddler you should be wary of severe pain which is accompanied by vomiting. This can be due to a serious condition in which the bowel telescopes up on itself (see *Intussusception*). In some cases, the baby passes blood-stained motions which look like redcurrant jelly.

Pain in the abdomen may also be due to an infection of the urinary tract (including the kidney), and this is more likely to occur in girls. See *Urinary problems*.

See also *Colic* in babies; and *Appendicitis*.

Beware of pain which *appears* to be in a little boy's tummy, but which is really in one of his testicles. This may be due to a 'torsion' (twisted testicle), which always needs an urgent operation.

But what are the common causes of abdominal pain?

Most cases of tummy ache in childhood are just due to indigestion or 'wind'. It's remarkably easy for a little bit of gas to get trapped in a sort of 'airlock' and give quite a bit of pain and discomfort until it manages to pass through.

Also remarkably common are cases of 'nervous tummy', in which the child responds to stress by producing a tummy ache. He's not making this up; he genuinely feels discomfort in his tummy (just like an adult's 'butterflies') whenever he's frightened or worried about something. For fairly obvious reasons, this kind of nervous stomach ache is more common on Monday mornings; when a child is in trouble at school; and when there are difficulties at home – particularly disputes between Mum and Dad.

Tummy ache is, of course, very common in association with those 'tummy bugs' which affect so many children. You know the sort of thing – a youngster picks up a germ and develops diarrhoea or vomiting, or both. In many cases, these symptoms are accompanied by abdominal pain – and very often the pain gets easier when the child has had a bowel motion.

There's another extremely common cause of tummy ache – but one which very few parents know about. It's this. When a youngster has an infection somewhere – particularly a throat infection or tonsillitis (see entry) – the little glands inside his tummy swell up 'in sympathy' – as part of the body's general reaction to the infection. This immediately produces abdominal discomfort and pain. The condition is called 'mesenteric adenitis'. It's not serious, and the discomfort will go away as the throat infection (or whatever) gets better.

What's the best way to manage a child's abdominal pain when you're not really sure what's causing it? Well, *don't* give him a laxative or aperient – which is what many people think you should do! This is the one action which could have serious consequences if there really were something nastily wrong inside your child's tum.

Instead, put the child to bed, with a nice warm 'hotty'. (Not, of course, in the case of a baby – since babies can be burned by hot water bottles). Keep her on fluids only – and if the pain goes on for more than two or three hours, give your doctor a ring and ask if the symptoms justify any further action.

Finally, *don't* make a big fuss about any childhood tummy ache. There is an unfortunate, though understandable, tendency for some children to notice the fact that abdominal pain can be a way of creating anxiety in adults! They are then liable to make a big deal of the occasional episodes of abdominal discomfort which (after all) all of us experience from time to time.

So, if you don't want your child to grow up being neurotic about his stomach (and if there are no indications of it being serious), just play it fairly cool when he says he's got a tummy ache.

ABRASIONS (Grazes)

Abrasions of the skin are jolly painful for the child, and every mother knows the experience of having a toddler scream the place down after having the skin scraped off his knees!

However, these painful but minor skin grazes will never give any serious trouble as long as you wash the child's skin carefully with soap and warm water, taking care to get rid of any gravel or dirt. Any of the standard proprietary antiseptics which you can buy from your chemist can then be applied. If the graze is extensive, you can dress it with an adhesive plaster. Or if it's very big, you can cover it with a square of sterile gauze.

Finally, remember that (although sweets are bad for the teeth) there's every excuse for giving the child a nice sweet after he's suffered an unpleasant and painful graze.

ABSCESSES

Abscesses are collections of pus. They can occur in various parts of the body – but in childhood the only common site is on the gums. These dental abscesses are due to infection getting into the gums through decayed teeth.

The classic symptom of a dental abscess is a painful swelling which develops quite suddenly on the gum. The only remedy is to take the child to a dentist, who will drain the abscess, probably also removing the decayed tooth.

ACCIDENTS

See *First Aid*.

ACNE

The word acne simply means any skin condition in which the skin is greasy and there are a lot of pimples, spots and blackheads (see picture below). Acne is very rare in younger children, but it

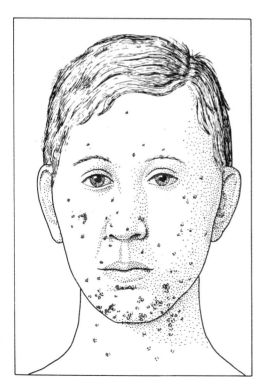

becomes more and more common as they get older – so much so that it is generally regarded by skin specialists as being not far short of universal in teenagers.

Acne is largely caused by changes in the balance of various hormones in the body, which is why it tends to develop after about the age of eleven or twelve, when sex hormones first start being produced in large quantities.

Good general measures include washing the face frequently, getting plenty of sunshine and fresh air, and avoiding touching or picking the nose – because the nose is a major source of germs! Squeezing pimples and spots should also be discouraged because this too will spread germs.

Nowadays, dermatologists don't feel that poor diet is a major cause of acne. Although there are various widely advertised remedies for acne, if the spots are particularly bad it's better to go and discuss the problem with your doctor, who may prescribe a course of antibiotics. The antibiotic which is usually chosen is one of the tetracycline group, and may have to be taken for many months. Exposure to ultraviolet light may help. So too may the application of steroid and antibiotic lotions to the skin.

Many doctors also prescribe agents for applying to the skin, such as benzoyl peroxide, sulphur, resorcinol, or tretinoin – a vitamin A derivative (not for under-12s).

ACUPUNCTURE

Acupuncture is a traditional Chinese treatment, in which the practitioner inserts fine needles into the patient's skin. A closely related form of therapy (practised by many acupuncturists) is moxibustion, in which little cones of material are allowed to smoulder on the skin at prescribed points.

Acupuncture is not used all that much for children in the UK – partly because the needles and the burning cones are liable to be frightening when you are young. However, there are a few conditions in which they may be useful in relieving pain.

How does acupuncture work? I have been to Hong Kong to investigate it, and have seen convincing evidence that it can help relieve pain – probably by stimulating the brain to release painkilling chemicals called 'endorphins'.

Most doctors now accept that acupuncture can be of real help in relieving pain. But the claim that it can be used to cure disease has not really been substantiated. In the West, doctors who have had high hopes of acupuncture's effect in treating disease have been rather disappointed in the last few years, because the results just don't seem to be forthcoming.

In practice, the main use of acupuncture among children is in helping to relieve the pain of those unfortunate kiddies who have long-standing painful illnesses such as arthritis (see *Arthritis*) or even cancer.

If you want your child to have acupuncture, it can be obtained in various ways. First, a child who is in severe, chronic pain, can be referred by her GP to one of the 170 or so Pain Clinics which are now run by the NHS – at many of which acupuncture is used by the doctors in charge.

Second, there is an excellent organization of medically qualified doctors who use acupuncture. Because of the strict rules of medical ethics, they will not actually recommend a particular doctor to you. However, if you write to them, they will send you a list of names and addresses in a sealed envelope, which they will ask you to take to your own doctor so that she can refer your child to a practitioner on the list. The address to write to is:

The British Medical Acupuncture
  Society
67–69 Chancery Lane
London WC2 1AF

There is another organization called The British Acupuncture Association. Its members are not necessarily doctors, but the Association has been in existence since 1961 and it does try to promote high standards of ethics and practice. The address to write to in order to find the name of a practitioner is:

The British Acupuncture Association
  & Register
c/o 19 Prebend Street
Leicester LE2 0LA

There are many freelance acupuncturists who advertise in local newspapers and so on. It's perfectly possible that most of them are sincere, and some of them may indeed be doing some good. But my own view is that unless you take a child to a member of a recognized professional association, there is certainly some risk that the acupuncturists might do more harm than good.

ADENOIDS

You hear a lot about children being 'adenoidal' or 'having adenoids'. In fact, *all* children have adenoids! The only trouble is that in some children the adenoids grow too big and may cause problems with breathing and with snoring.

The adenoids are small pads of lymphatic tissue (i.e. gland tissue) which are found at the back of the cavity of your child's nose just above her palate. They are usually quite large in young children, so they may cause some degree of obstruction to the passage of air through the cavity at the back of the nose. If they get very big, then the child will tend to snore a lot and to speak with that familiar adenoidal, 'blocked up' sort of voice.

A lot of youngsters grow out of this phase without any treatment. However, others have to have their adenoids removed – via the throat – usually at the same time that the tonsils are taken out. (See *Tonsillitis* and *Tonsillectomy*.)

There is now widespread feeling among doctors that both adenoids and tonsils were taken out much too frequently in the past. An operation is always an ordeal for a child, and I'm afraid there's always the slight risk of something going wrong. If your GP can control the symptoms of your child's adenoid problems with nose drops or antibiotics, then that's better than having to undergo an operation.

AIR SICKNESS

See *Travel sickness*.

ALLERGIES

Allergies are far more common than doctors used to think – I have about half a dozen myself! Many children are allergic to such things as pollen, animal hairs, tiny mites in house dust, feathers, drugs or food colourings.

Symptoms which allergies produce are very varied, but common manifestations include asthma, hayfever, some types of eczema and dermatitis, and urticaria (nettle rash). Very occasionally allergies may even cause collapse and unconsciousness.

What happens in an allergic reaction? Well, the child's body is exposed to an agent called an antigen. Although this antigen produces no obvious ill effects on the first occasion, the child's tissues produce substances called antibodies in response. On the next occasion that his body is exposed to the same antigen (whether it's grass or tree pollen, animal hair or skin scales or some type of food), the union of antigen and antibody is liable to produce dramatic effects, such as a severe skin rash, an asthma attack or a bout of hayfever-type symptoms.

In many families there is a marked hereditary tendency to allergic conditions – particularly eczema, hayfever, dust-mite allergy and asthma. In some of these families, a child who has eczema as a baby may develop hayfever and/or asthma as he grows older.

Happily, new methods of treatment are making things easier for the allergic child. These include newer antihistamine drugs (which do not cause sedation, like the old anti-histamines), desensitization techniques and other methods to protect the child's body tissues against allergies. These treatments are discussed under the following headings: *Asthma*; *Dust allergy*; *Eczema*; and *Hayfever*.

ALOPECIA

Alopecia just means baldness. Unfortunately, a few children (for reasons which are not understood) develop unusual forms of childhood baldness. One form is called alopecia areata, and the other is called alopecia totalis.

Alopecia areata is more common. In this condition, there are only small localized patches of hair loss (see picture below). It may occur some months after an illness or an emotional upset. Fortunately, in many children the hair regrows after a few months. It's important to distinguish this condition from ringworm (see *Ringworm*), which quite often gives a similar appearance.

Alopecia totalis is fortunately rare. In this disorder there is loss of *all* the hair on the head, often including the eyebrows. A typical case was that of the famous swimmer Duncan Mayhew. Unfortunately, the cause of the condition is not known, and the outlook for regrowth of hair is not all that good.

Baldness also occurs in children who are being treated with strong chemical agents because they have some form of cancer or leukaemia. Although the total loss of hair is very dramatic and often very upsetting for them (and nearly always distressing for their parents) there is an excellent chance that the hair will grow back normally again.

ALTERNATIVE MEDICINE

There's a greatly increased interest in alternative (or complementary) medicine these days. This is partly because orthodox medicine so often fails to produce good results that many people have become disenchanted with it. This doesn't, in my view, alter the fact that for most childhood disorders, orthodox medicine almost certainly is the best thing.

However, I do agree with the increasingly widespread view that we doctors have tended to use far too many powerful drugs on both children and adults in recent years. If we can find a natural remedy without serious side-effects to treat a childhood disorder, then there's much obviously to be said for it.

Warning. Anyone can set himself up as a practitioner of alternative medicine – and the fact has to be faced that some of those who stick up plates outside their houses or who advertise in local newspapers are charlatans! Others may be very sincere, but have absolutely no training and might well do your child some harm.

So I personally am all in favour of making sure that, if you use an alternative practitioner for your child, the practitioner is a member of a recognized professional body which insists on good standards of training, practice and ethics. I think it's fair to say that the alternative disciplines have been a bit slow in getting their act together and forming such professional bodies, but it's certainly happening now – and there are reliable professional associations which govern the practice of the major alternative therapies.

The alternative methods of treatment which I've discussed in this book are: *Acupuncture; Chiropractic; Clinical Ecology; Herbalism; Homoeopathy; Hypnotism; Naturopathy* and *Osteopathy*. As well as giving separate entries for each of these. I've tried to include brief mention of complementary remedies under the various major childhood ailments listed in the book.

Please bear in mind that with nearly all types of complementary medicine, it's almost impossible to make a scientific analysis of exactly what percentage of children will respond to the therapy – or even whether it works at all! So except in a very few instances, I haven't *recommended* any particular line of alternative treatment. It's up to you to decide whether you think it would be suitable for your family.

ANAEMIA

Anaemia means weakness of the blood. This is usually due to lack of iron – but can sometimes be due to other causes.

Lack of iron can be caused by:
a   inadequate intake of iron in food
b   loss of iron because of bleeding.

In fact, anaemia is *not* very common in children. This is because the main causes of heavy blood loss (e.g. prolonged periods, or bleeding ulcers) occur in adults, and not in children.

But iron-deficiency anaemia does occur in some babies and toddlers, because both breast milk and cow's milk are lacking in iron. A healthy full-term baby has acquired from its mother enough iron stores to last him for the first six months of life. However, if his mother was a bit anaemic, he may not really have had a chance to collect enough iron from her.

The same thing may happen with premature babies, and with twins – who have to share their mother's iron between them! In children of any age, iron deficiency may be due to a diet which is lacking in iron – so there is every reason to encourage youngsters to eat plenty of meat and fish, which are rich in this mineral. (Contrary to what many parents believe, spinach is *not* a particularly good source of iron!)

The *symptoms* of anaemia are paleness, tiredness, and sometimes breathlessness. In some children, there may be an odd tendency to eat strange 'foods' – such as ice!

The *treatment* of iron-deficiency anaemia is simply to replace the iron with iron-containing medicines. The results of this are very good indeed.

For other occasional causes of anaemia in children see *Sickle-cell anaemia*, and *Leukaemia*.

APPENDICITIS

Appendicitis means inflammation of the appendix – a small organ located in the lower right-hand corner of your child's tummy, as you can see from the illustration

The appendix is about the size and shape of a small worm. Fortunately, it has no known function, and therefore it doesn't matter if it has to be removed.

The actual cause of appendicitis is not known. There have been suggestions that it might be due to the rather unhealthy diet we eat in the West, but this remains unproven.

There's about a one in ten chance that your child will have his appendix removed one day. So this operation, called 'appendicectomy' (or 'appendectomy' if you're American), is one of the most common of all surgical procedures. Some 83,000 appendixes are taken out each year in this country – and if they were laid end to end they'd stretch from Buckingham Palace to St Paul's and back again!

Appendix removal is a very safe operation, though all 'ops' do of course carry a slight risk. If your child gets appendicitis one day, there is no need for you to worry, since she's almost certain to come through it OK.

But let me make clear at the outset that it would be unusual for your child to develop appendicitis during babyhood – only a very few babies get it. However, once toddlerhood is reached, the incidence begins to rise, and it's really quite common among children of playschool age – and more so among schoolboys and schoolgirls.

The classic symptoms of appendicitis are as follows:

- tummy pain increasing over several hours
- loss of interest in food
- vomiting – but rarely more than once or twice
- a very off-colour feeling
- a moderately raised temperature (though this is variable).

On the question of pain: people are always worried about tummy aches, in case they signal appendicitis. In fact, the great majority of tummy aches don't indicate anything of the kind. (See *Abdominal pain.*) By and large, it's only if a tummy pain has gone on for several hours that you need to start thinking of appendicitis. In general, appendix pain tends to start in the central part of the stomach, and then to shift down to the lower right-hand corner after a few hours. But I must stress that there are many, many variants to this pattern. So if in doubt, you have to be guided by your own doctor.

If your GP thinks that the child might have acute appendicitis, he'll get him into hospital. Once there, he'll be examined again and assessed by the hospital doctors. In fact, by the time a child is settled down into a hospital bed, the pain which was *thought* to have been due to appendicitis has very often settled down. In these cases, of course, no operation is necessary.

If your child really has got acute appendicitis, he'll be taken to the operating theatre, gently eased off to sleep by the anaesthetist, and then operated on. As a rule, the operation itself is totally straightforward. The surgeon makes a small incision, about one and a half to two inches long (or about four to five centimetres if you like). Then he probes down through the muscle layers of the tummy, so that he can get access to the abdominal cavity. Once inside, he finds the inflamed appendix, fishes it out of the hole, clamps it at its base (to prevent leakage) and then cuts it off. Finally, he ties a small 'purse-string' stitch round the stump of the appendix (again, to prevent leakage into the abdominal cavity) before stitching up the muscle and the skin. Then the child goes back to the ward to recover.

Obviously, he'll feel a bit 'woozy' when he comes round, but he shouldn't be in a lot of pain – and what pain he does have will soon go away. In a few hours, he'll probably be thinking about food again – and by next day he'll very likely be running around the ward. It won't be long before he's home – and back to school or playschool. But he must take it easy for a couple of weeks (in other words, *not* play football or fight!) because his stomach will be tender for a fortnight or so.

An appendix incision usually needs only a few stitches (or sometimes metal clips). These are usually taken out about a week or so after the operation. The process is very nearly painless, incidentally.

Up till now we've been talking about the acute illness, where the child has a highly inflamed appendix and is really quite ill. But there's another common situation in which the appendix is removed – when a child is said to have a non-acute or 'grumbling' appendix – in other words, one that just gives a little pain from time to time over a period of months or years.

In fact, many doctors are doubtful whether the 'grumbling appendix' condition exists at all. They think that it's a mistake to attribute the odd aches and pains in the tummy – which can be due to a variety of causes – to the appendix,

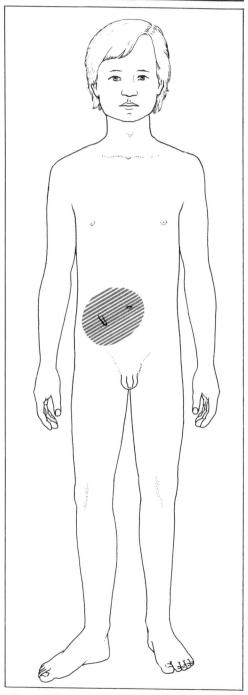

Where your child's appendix is – and (in red) the area where pain usually occurs

especially as the appearance of the organ in such cases is usually quite normal.

However, other doctors disagree. If a child keeps getting pain in the right-hand lower corner of the tummy over a long period, they will make a diagnosis of 'chronic' or 'grumbling' appendicitis, and arrange for the child to come in and be operated on as a non-emergency case.

Since the procedure is not an emergency, this type of elective appendicectomy is even safer than emergency appendicectomy.

ARTHRITIS

Yes, children *do* sometimes get arthritis. It's usually a juvenile form of the well-known adult condition called 'rheumatoid arthritis' (see *Rheumatoid arthritis; Still's disease*).

ASPIRIN

Aspirin is an extremely useful drug, and many parents have found it a great help to give it to their children when they're a bit feverish. There are however some dangers associated with it. In the UK (though not in many other countries), official advice since 1986 has been that it should only be given to under-twelves in rare circumstances, because of the risk of Reye's syndrome (see *Reye's syndrome*).

Aspirin lowers the temperature, combats inflammation and relieves pain.

Many parents don't realize that a lot of the proprietary painkilling prepara-

tions on the market do in fact merely consist of aspirin (or aspirin with another ingredient). Check the small print on the packet. If it does, it will usually have written on it in small letters the words 'acetyl salicylic acid'. Below is a list of some common aspirin-containing products.

Some common aspirin-containing products

Do *not* give these to your child because of the possible risk of Reye's syndrome.

Alka Seltzer	Beecham's
Anadin	Powders
Aspirin Tablets	Disprin
(whether Junior,	Hypon
Ordinary or	Phensic
Soluble)	Solprin
Aspro	Veganin

The cheapest way to buy aspirin is in the form of 'Aspirin BP'. Despite the claims of the manufacturers, it's a little doubtful as to whether the more expensive brands of aspirin-containing tablet really have any significant advantage.

Junior aspirin were withdrawn in the UK in 1986 because of the Reye's syndrome alarm, but unfortunately many people will have them in their houses for some years to come. They are dangerously attractive to children! Do bear in mind that even these junior aspirin tablets are poisonous – and that in overdose they can and do kill children. It's far from unknown for a child to swallow a handful of junior aspirin because she liked the look of those nice sweeties! All aspirin tablets (in whatever form) should be carefully locked up in a safe place where children cannot get at them in any circumstances. By doing this you may prevent a tragedy.

The great majority of children over the age of eleven can safely be given aspirin tablets. But don't give them to a younger child unless your doctor says so. And because of the risk of Reye's syndrome, never give them in cases of chickenpox or 'flu.

I have to make absolutely clear that aspirin is a *drug* – contrary to what many people may think. This means that it can have side effects, and that very rarely those side effects can be extremely serious.

The most common side effect of aspirin is irritation of the stomach – this may cause tummy ache, or even internal bleeding. For this reason, aspirin shouldn't be used to treat tummy ache.

Official advice is that aspirin should also be used with caution in children and young people with asthma (because it can cause spasm of the air tubes),

ASTHMA

This is a common chest disorder in childhood. It's characterized by intermittent bouts of wheezing and breathlessness, which are due to temporary narrowing of the air passages leading to your child's lungs, and also to partial blockage of these passages by mucus or inflammatory swelling.

To get an idea of how unpleasant it is for a child to be in the grip of an asthmatic attack, hold your half-closed fist in front of your mouth with the circle created by your thumb and forefinger held against your lips – so that there's a wide 'tube' you can breathe through. Now, breathing only through your mouth, start clenching your fist a bit tighter . . . and then tighter still. Can you feel the effort you have to make to drag the air in? Can you hear the alarming sound it makes as it whistles through the rapidly closing tube? Are you beginning to panic slightly as you realize that your supply of air is being cut off?

That's how a child feels when he has an attack of asthma. Once his chest starts wheezing and he finds he's fighting for air, it's no wonder he's scared for his life.

Some parents tend to be irritated by a child who's having a bad attack of the wheezes. 'Oh come now,' they say, 'pull yourself together. It's not as bad as all that, surely.' But asthma is a frightening and dangerous business and the child who's suffering from an attack is not putting it on.

What causes asthma? There are three main factors: allergy, infection and stress, of which the first is by far the most important. Infection plays a modest part, and stress a very minor one.

Allergy is an irrational defence reaction by the body to some outside stimulus: a protective reaction gone wrong, in fact. The child comes in contact with something he is allergic to and his air passages start closing down almost as if making a desperate attempt to keep out the allergen (see *Allergies*).

There's now some evidence that breast-feeding during the first few months of life helps to prevent a baby from developing an allergy. This is particularly important when parents have allergies themselves.

If a young baby who has an allergic tendency is given cow's milk (and all bottle-feeds are cow's milk) it seems that the foreign protein in the milk may trigger off a long-lasting allergy such as asthma or eczema.

Infection is the second trigger of asthma. All children get colds and coughs, and if the infection spreads to the chest in a child with an allergic or wheezy tendency, often the air passages become inflamed. The lining of these tubes becomes swollen, which makes them narrower inside. And they also pour out mucus – which bungs things up even further.

So a chest infection may trigger quite a bad asthmatic attack. If your child has asthma you need to be able to recognize the signs of a cold or sore throat 'going to the chest'; when this starts to happen you should take him to the doctor so that if necessary he can be put on antibiotics.

There's some argument about the part stress plays in asthma. Probably the role of psychological factors has been exaggerated in the past. It's also important to remember that asthma is a stressful illness. If you had frequent alarming attacks in which you had to fight for breath, then you'd probably end up a bit tense too! In other words, though asthmatic children do tend to be more highly-strung than others, it may well be the disease that has caused the stress rather than the other way round.

I wouldn't deny that many asthmatics (particularly children) seem to get wheezier when they're thwarted. It's also true that most doctors have seen people in an asthmatic attack improve dramatically when they're given what they're told is a powerful injection – which is in fact only distilled water! But parents should always remember that a child having a bad asthmatic attack has a serious physical condition which needs urgent treatment.

If your child has asthma, or even just the borderline asthma of a wheezy chest, you should begin by trying to identify the allergen. You may not succeed, but it's worth a try. Pollen, house dust, animal dander (shed skin cells) and moulds are all possible causes. And they're causes which you can do something about – for instance, avoid contact with cats or even move to a less dusty house.

In the last few years, it's become apparent that certain foods can sometimes provoke allergy and hence asthma attacks. These include milk, eggs, cheese, coffee and food additives such as tartrazine (a yellow dye). Your GP or a specialist can advise you about excluding certain items of food from your child's diet to try to find out what's provoking the attacks.

Unfortunately, identifying the allergen is largely a question of trial and error. Skin tests for allergy can be arranged at special centres but they aren't all that reliable. Home trial and error is often just as good. For instance, if a girl is always wheezy when she wakes up in her bedroom but fine when she's out in the open air, it's a fair bet that she's allergic to house dust.

Certainly the evidence would seem to suggest that asthmatic children who go away to school often get much better – and this may, of course, be due to the fact that boarding school takes a child away from possible allergens in his own home, not to mention psychological stresses within the family.

Most chest specialists believe that it's good for asthmatic or wheezy children to lead an active, energetic life. You should make every effort not to mollycoddle a wheezy child. Encourage him to take part in sports and rough-and-tumbles with his mates, and don't let him regard himself as an invalid.

Modern drug therapy is often very effective. There are various anti-asthma drugs which have been given in tablet or medicine form for many years. These open up the child's airways if an attack seems to be developing.

Aerosol inhalers, which contain rather more sophisticated 'tube-widening' drugs, have been prescribed since about 1960. Your child's GP, chest physician or paediatrician will advise you on how often to use the aerosol.

Steroids, or cortisone-like drugs, are powerful anti-inflammatory agents, and so can damp down the wild allergic reaction in the lungs which is characteristic of asthma. These pills can also be dangerous, and long-term use inevitably leads to dependence and (especially in children) to severe side effects. For that reason doctors are rather wary about putting children – or anybody else – on steroid pills such as predisone or prednisolone, except when the asthma is really bad. In a severe attack, however, steroids can be life-saving, so they must be used.

It's worrying that some asthmatics who die in an attack haven't had steroids – often because they haven't reached hospital soon enough. So if your child has a really bad attack, you should seek medical advice rapidly so that steroids can be given by injection if they're needed. If your GP is away and it looks as though you'll have to wait hours for a deputizing service to arrive, it may be best to take your child directly to the nearest hospital accident and emergency department, where steroids and other treatment can be given.

There are several newer drugs which have made a great impact on the treatment of asthma. The main ones are: Intal (cromoglycate); Becotide (beclomethasone); and Zaditen (ketotifen). These drugs are intended to *prevent* attacks, not to treat an attack once it's started. On some occasions parents have abandoned them as being 'no good' because they don't relieve an attack.

Becotide is an inhaled aerosol steroid, but doesn't carry the dangers of steroids given by mouth or injection. Intal is a powder taken in through a special inhaler (the Spinhaler). Its function is to coat the allergy cells in the lungs with a protective blockade which keeps the allergens from getting to them. It must be used three to four times a day. Some parents actually open the capsules and scatter the powder on the child's pillow so he can inhale it while he sleeps. This is OK. Zaditen – a newer drug – is claimed to provide long-term protection for the allergy cells of the lung. It also has a more general anti-allergy effect, and, like many anti-allergy drugs, may cause sleepiness.

So, an ever-widening range of anti-asthma drugs – plus the new understanding of how certain allergies can trigger off attacks – does mean that the outlook for the wheezy or asthmatic child is better than it's ever been before. She may well grow out of it, but if she doesn't, then it's likely that the drugs now available will keep the severity and frequency of her attacks down to a reasonable and tolerable level for her, and her parents.

Alternative therapy
In asthma, **homoeopaths** tend to use remedies such as phosphorus, nux

vomica, sulphur and ipecacuanha (see *Homoeopathy*). **Acupuncturists** tend to use both needling and moxibustion (see *Acupuncture*) to try to open up the bronchial tubes. **Naturopaths** believe that constitutional treatment with dietetic guidance is of benefit in asthma (see *Naturopathy*). Like the **clinical ecologists**, they would (quite reasonably) try and identify foods and other allergens to which the asthmatic child might be abnormally sensitive (see *Clinical Ecology*).

Do *not* use an imported Asian alternative remedy called Dumcaps or Duzcaps. These are alleged to be homoeopathic, but in fact contain powerful steroid drugs.

ATHLETE'S FOOT

This is a fungus infection of the skin, very common among older children – especially boys. It spreads rapidly among youngsters who go barefoot on moist floors. So it's often picked up in showers, games changing rooms, bathrooms, dormitories, and so on.

The fungus, for some unknown reason, almost invariably attacks the gap between the fourth and the fifth toe, though it may spread to other toes, to the sole of the foot, and often to the crutch area.

There's really not a lot of point in taking your child to the doctor if he gets athlete's foot, since your local chemist will sell you perfectly satisfactory and inexpensive remedies. I find that a good and very cheap one is the traditional Whitfield's ointment, but there are also many proprietary preparations.

For as long as your child has athlete's foot, try and encourage him not to wander round the house barefoot! He should try and get his slippers on as soon as he has stepped out of the bath and dried his feet. Socks should be changed every day. Do *not* let him pick between his toes, as this can only help the fungus to spread around the house!

AUTISM

Autism is an uncommon but extremely distressing disorder, in which a young child seems to live completely in a world of his own.

The cause, unfortunately, is unknown. Parents tend to blame themselves when they have an autistic child, but in fact this isn't justifiable. No one has the faintest idea what causes this sad condition.

The characteristic thing about the autistic child is his aloofness from other people: he really wants nothing whatever to do with them. He usually shows no love for his parents nor for anyone else, and takes no pleasure in other people's company. This isn't his fault – there is clearly something very wrong with his mind.

I'm afraid that there's no medicine which will cure autism. The main hope is to educate the child to achieve a more normal method of behaviour. To do this, you will need the help of a child psychiatry unit with experience in dealing with autism. Therapists usually try to find some way of establishing contact with the autistic child – which will be very difficult. Speech therapy is important too.

The strain on the parents of an autistic child is invariably enormous. If your child is autistic, then you should definitely get in contact with:

The National Society for Autistic
Children
276, Willesden Lane
London NW2

whose help and support can be invaluable.

BACKACHE

Fortunately, backache is not very common in children. Most cases are due to minor strains, and are not of great significance. Disc trouble is most unusual in childhood.

However, some children do develop backache as a result of a condition called osteochondritis. This is when a small area of bone inside the spine is destroyed so that the child develops pain and sometimes a round-shouldered posture. The condition is also known as Scheuermann's disease.

But however impressive the name, I'm afraid we don't know what causes it. Treatment is usually by a course of exercises. Children who suffer from this form of osteochondritis are usually advised to refrain from violent sports, such as Rugby or football, for a while.

Alternative therapy
Backache is one area of medicine where alternative techniques often do prove a great deal better than orthodox ones. If your child has recurrent backache which doesn't seem to be responding to orthodox methods, then it probably would be worth getting an appointment with either an **osteopath** or a **chiropractor** (see *Osteopathy* and *Chiropractic*).

But manipulation is not – repeat NOT – a good idea in cases of osteochondritis (see above).

Finally, I should mention that **clinical ecologists** believe that food exclusion can sometimes cause enormous improvements in cases of backache. I find this a bit hard to believe.

BAD BREATH

Bad breath (halitosis) in children is nearly always due to some problem with the teeth. Parents often worry that it's due to something wrong inside the child's stomach or intestines, but this is not very likely when you consider that the breath comes out of the lungs and not the stomach! Constipation is *not* a cause of bad breath, as many parents believe. However, bad breath does occur very frequently during an attack of acute appendicitis, and in other conditions where a child has a raised temperature.

Usually, though, bad breath has a much more mundane cause. As it passes through the child's mouth it's all too easy for the breath to pick up unpleasant pongs from areas of decay, or from bits of food matter left behind in the teeth. (Sorry if this doesn't sound very pleasant!)

So the first thing to do if you notice that your child has bad breath is to make sure that he cleans his teeth at least twice a day. If this doesn't solve the problem, the next thing to do is to take him to the dentist and let her check him out for any signs of decay or gum disease.

If the dentist gives the child a clean bill of health, but you're still worried about his breath, don't make a big thing about it. Just ensure that he goes on cleaning his teeth, and encourage him to use a mouth wash once a day – for instance a proprietary preparation such as Listerine (called after the famous anti-septic surgeon, Joseph Lister. If they hadn't called it 'Listerine', they'd have to have called it 'Josephine').

BAT EARS

Bat ears (or jug ears) are unusually prominent ears. This can be a very trying affliction for a child, because he's often teased about it at school or play-school. Sometimes the condition runs in the family. The actual cause is not known. It's *not* caused by sleeping with the ears folded forward during baby-hood, as a lot of people imagine.

If the condition is really severe, then you should talk to your doctor about taking your child to a plastic surgeon. The operation to cure bat ears is very minor, and just involves removing some tissue from behind the ears, so as to pin them back. It's likely that you would be able to get this done on the NHS rather than having to pay for it privately.

BED-WETTING

Bed-wetting (or nocturnal enuresis) causes children – and parents – a great deal of grief.

This is a pity, because all this tension and trauma is usually quite unneces-sary; very often dads and mums expect far too much of their children in the night-time dryness department.

There's an adult tendency to expect children to be dry much too early, and to get far too emotionally upset when they don't oblige by being dry as early as hoped for.

Even today there are plenty of parents who still punish a child for bed-wetting (or at least tell him off severely); this is crazy because the child doesn't mean to do it. There really is nothing he'd like better than to be able to stop wetting the bed.

Never expect too much from a youngster. I'm always amazed when parents of three-year-olds or even two-year-olds walk into a doctor's surgery complaining about bed-wetting. It's perfectly *normal* at that age.

If your child is dry at night at the age of two, then you're very lucky – and he's very unusual. But even at the age of four, half the youngsters in Britain are still sometimes wet at night. And a very substantial proportion of five-year-olds are still wet: this is natural for them, even if it's rather tough on Mum, who is usually the one who has to wash the sheets.

Only after the age of five is there any point in seeking medical treatment for a child's bed-wetting. Yet large numbers of parents of two- or three-year-old children take them to the doctor and demand powerful (and dangerous) medicines in an effort to make their poor kids dry. So I'll say it again: if your child is still wet at night at age three or four, accept it as normal. Stick a waterproof sheet on his bed and try to forget about it.

OK, but what about children of five and a half, six or seven who keep wet-ting? Clearly, you have to take some action about this.

First, don't assume – as so many

people do – that drugs are the answer. The drugs which are used in an effort to combat bed-wetting are actually the powerful mind-affecting agents which many adults take for depression – for instance, Tofranil (imipramine) and Tryptizol (amitriptyline).

In theory, they are supposed to alter the child's level of consciousness while he's sleeping, and so make him more likely to wake up when his bladder's full. In practice, it doesn't work very well. While some children appear to get better on these drugs, others don't. And even when they do get better, you can't be sure that it wasn't just a question of growing up, so that his night-time bladder control improved anyway.

But the most worrying thing about these drugs is that they're supplied as pleasant-tasting fruit-flavoured syrups. So it's not surprising that kids sometimes get at them and have an extra swig. Yet such drugs can kill – and in Britain they're the commonest cause of fatal poisoning in young children these days.

If you really feel you want to try the drugs out on your child, for heaven's sake make sure you lock them away. Otherwise, you may end up not with a dry child, but with a dead one.

Parents often try to combat wetting by 'lifting' – that is, taking the child out of bed once or twice during the night and holding him over the loo until, in a dazed sort of way, he wees. Nowadays, many doctors seem to advise against this, but I believe it's a harmless practice, and it probably does prevent at least some wet beds.

Restricting fluid is another widely used practice. The idea is that if you don't let your child have any fluid in the later part of the evening, she'll be less likely to pee during the night. This doesn't seem to be wildly successful, and it is certainly cruel if you overdo the fluid restriction. Personally, I think that while it is common sense to prevent your child from knocking back three mugs of cocoa just before she goes to bed, it's unkind to deprive her of *any* drinks in the evening.

A 'star chart' is an 'encouragement trick' which has become popular in recent years. Every time he's dry the child can stick a gold star on a large calendar in his room. Some people swear by this method, but it's a little hard to see the virtue of it, since the poor kid has no conscious control of what his bladder does while he's asleep anyway. If you do use the star chart, make sure that you don't make the child feel a failure every time he's wet. Also, you must take care that his friends don't see your youngster's chart and realize his problem – children can be very cruel about this sort of thing!

Now to the best way of treating bed-wetting – alarms. These entirely safe devices work by means of a special electrical pad under your child's sheet. If he passes just the tiniest drop of pee during the night, that drop will complete an electrical circuit which runs through the pad. It's a bit like the pad of a burglar alarm, in fact. The battery-powered circuit is connected to a buzzer which is placed by his bed, and the completion of the circuit sets off the buzzer – and it's so loud that it'll wake any child! Naturally, you'll have told the youngster that he's to get up and go to the loo when he hears the buzzer.

In a majority of cases this treatment will cure the child of bed-wetting within a few months. It can't cure *all* cases, but it's often successful where drugs and star charts have failed. And there are no side effects.

Some paediatric and child health clinics have bought alarms like this for lending out to parents. But by and large, you have to buy or rent your own. Here are the addresses of some firms who either sell or hire out these alarms:

Astric Products Ltd, Lewes Road, Brighton BN2 3LG

F. Gulliver Devices Ltd, The Mews, 49/51 Station Road, London E4 7UJ

N. H. Eastwood & Son Ltd, 70 Nursery Road, Southgate, London N14 9QH

Wessex Medical Equipment Co., 108 The Hundred, Romsey, Southampton, Hants

Rehab Ltd, 17, Ludlow Hill, Melton Road, West Bridgford, Nottingham NG2 6HD

By the way, remember that quite a lot of children who wet the bed do so because of some emotional problem. They may be worried about a bully at school, or about rows at home – but, without meaning to, they respond to whatever psychological stress is affecting them by wetting themselves at night.

If your child has been dry for a year or two but then inexplicably becomes wet again, it's likely that this is due to some psychological stress. Obviously, you owe it to him to try to find out what it is.

Finally, an appreciable proportion of children who are very late bed-wetters do turn out to have some internal structural abnormality of the waterworks, and sometimes a urinary infection (see *Urinary problems*).

So if your youngster has reached the age of eight or more and is still wetting, it may well be worth seeing a paediatrician, who could decide whether special x rays of the urinary tract are necessary.

As these aren't a lot of fun for the child, I wouldn't advise parents to rush into having them done. But they do sometimes reveal some abnormality which might be put right by surgery, and this may cure the bed-wetting.

Note: If everything has failed and your youngster is *still* wetting at the age of eleven, twelve or even older, don't give up hope. There's a steady spontaneous cure rate with each year of increasing age. Many children who've been their mums' despair suddenly and inexplicably become dry one night – and never wet themselves again.

Alternative therapy

Homoeopaths tend to treat bed-wetting with remedies such as belladonna, arsenic and lycopodium. **Clinical ecologists** believe that an exclusion diet (particularly exclusion of cow's milk) is helpful.

Bee stings

See *First Aid*.

Belching

Belching or burping in childhood is hardly ever due to any physical disease or abnormality. An occasional burp is quite normal in children (and especially in babies!).

Repeated and uncontrollable burping in youngsters is nearly always due to nerves. The child who is tense or anxious (as often happens with adults too) responds by swallowing air. Her stomach can only hold a limited quantity of air (not much more than a large tumblerful, in fact). So the inevitable result is that within a very short time, up it comes! The poor child very often responds to this embarrassment by promptly swallowing some more air – so producing more burps.

Obviously, the youngster doesn't mean to do this, so it is quite pointless to get cross with her. As no drug is likely to help the situation, by far the best thing is not to make a fuss, and instead to try and reassure her that all is well. As with so many other nervous habits, if you can find out what is causing the child's tenseness, the habit will go away.

BILIOUSNESS

This is an old term which you may hear grandparents use about children ('I think your little Johnny's a bit bilious today').

Up until twenty or thirty years ago it was widely thought that abdominal pain or discomfort in children was often due to something wrong with the bile (the digestive liquid produced by the liver). It's now known that this isn't so. In fact, there's no such thing as biliousness.

(For causes of abdominal pain, see *Abdominal pain*.)

BIRTHMARKS

Nearly all children have some sort of mark present on the skin at birth. Fortunately, well over 90 per cent of these marks are so small or unnoticeable that they don't cause any distress.

Many of the rest are only a centimetre or two across, and are on parts of the body where they don't matter very much. If your child has a small mark like this, then all you need to do is to reassure her that it's of no significance.

However, about five children in every hundred do have bigger marks (or marks located on the face) which cause them and their parents a lot of distress.

Happily, some types of birthmarks do shrink in the most astonishing way during the first few years of life – and your GP or child health clinic doctor may well be able to reassure you that your child has this type of shrinking mark.

If not, what can be done? First, do your level best not to go on about the mark within earshot of the child. Also, reassure her that, though it is noticeable, it doesn't make her different from anyone else, or 'inferior' in any way – and that you love her just the same!

Ugly marks can be dealt with either by surgery or by camouflage with make-up. Most unpleasant scars and many birthmarks can be removed by plastic surgeons these days. However, you may well find that your child's doctors are not keen to rush into operating on him, for several reasons.

First, as the birthmark might shrink right down surgery may not be needed at all. Second, a small child is usually difficult to operate on from a technical point of view. The bigger she gets, the easier it is to refashion the blemished area of her skin. So again, the surgeon may prefer to delay as long as possible. Third, doctors do realize (and I'm afraid most other people do not) that there is a definite risk from any surgical operation.

Unless doctors are fairly sure of a good result from the operation, they may well advise the alternative course of camouflaging the lesion with make-up. In the UK this can often be prescribed under the NHS. If your child's blemish or scar is bad enough for her to have to go to see a plastic surgeon, the surgeon will advise you about make-up and one of his team will probably show you how to use it. Alternatively (see below) the firm which manufactures the make-up may well be happy to give you advice. Your local branch of the Red Cross can sometimes show you the best way to use these products to cover up your child's scar or birthmark.

Even very large marks can be covered using these techniques and most parents (and doctors) are amazed by the way in which a disfigurement can be made to disappear completely or almost completely.

If your child has only a small mark which is a nuisance but which obviously doesn't require a specialized opinion, your GP will probably be the person you'll turn to for advice. It is not always realized that GPs can sometimes prescribe camouflaging make-up under the NHS. These types of make-up are classified as 'borderline substances' – which broadly speaking means that the GP can prescribe them only in cases of genuine need.

If your doctor prescribes them for your child on an NHS prescription form (which he has to mark with certain special 'code' initials), they will of course be free. But you can also buy them over the counter.

BITES

See *Dog bites*; *Snake bites*; *Wasp* and *Bee stings* (in the *First Aid* section).

BLACKHEADS

These are collections of oily material in the pores of a child's skin. They can be pressed out with a special instrument called a comedone extractor, obtainable from chemists.

Blackheads are, of course, often an early sign of acne (see *Acne*).

Brand	Maker	Notes
Dermacolor	C. H. Fox Ltd 22 Tavistock Sq. London WC2	Cream and fixing powder
Covermark	Stiefel Ltd Wooburn Green High Wycombe Bucks	Masking cream (10 shades) spotstick (7 shades) powder (1 shade) rouge (3 shades) shading cream grey toner
Keromask	Innoxa 202 Terminus Rd Eastbourne E. Sussex	8 shades: 3 base & 5 toning
Veil Cover Cream	Thomas Blake & Co. 20 Blatchford Close Horsham W. Sussex	14 natural skin shades, including 'ethnic' ones

BLADDER PROBLEMS

See *Urinary problems*.

BLEEDING

See *First Aid*.

BOILS

Many children get recurrent boils, especially if they're run down or (for some reason) if they're overweight. If your youngster keeps on getting boils, then you should take her to the doctor for a check-up. You should also take along a specimen of urine, so that the doctor can check it for sugar. This is because recurrent boils can occasionally indicate diabetes.

Treatment of boils is unfortunately a bit unsatisfactory. Many doctors prescribe antibiotics, but it's doubtful whether the antibiotic can really penetrate the 'wall' around the boil and do any good.

The traditional treatment of trying to 'draw' the boil with a magnesium sulphate dressing is probably as good as anything, and certainly does no harm.

A boil which has actually developed a 'head' on it can often be lanced by your doctor. What you should *not* do is to squeeze your child's boil yourself – this is just likely to spread germs to other parts of his skin (and possibly to you as well).

BOWELS

Parents get a bit muddled by the word bowels, because they're often not entirely sure what a 'bowel' is. Really, the word means the same as 'intestines' – in other words the very long stretch of tubing which leads from the child's stomach to his bottom.

As you can see from the picture, this tubing is divided into two parts: the small intestine (or small bowel) –

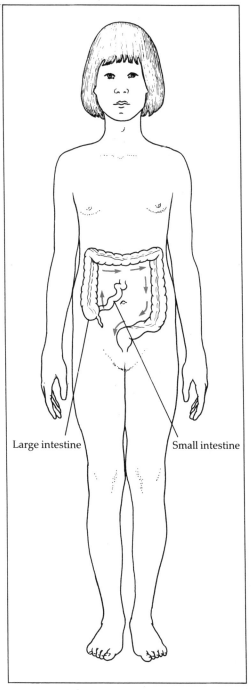

Large intestine   Small intestine

Arrows show direction of waste matter (motions) passing down to rectum

through the wall of which the child absorbs nourishment from the food; and the large intestine (large bowel) – which acts as a reservoir for the waste matter left over after the nutriment has been extracted.

Of course, in ordinary speech the word bowels tends to be used in connection with passing bowel *motions*. For problems in this area, see *Constipation* and *Diarrhoea*.

BOW LEGS

Bow legs (or genu varum) are, thank heavens, much less common than they used to be – because of the virtual eradication of rickets from Britain.

However, rickets does still occasionally occur – particularly in Asian children in sun-starved northern cities – and there are other causes of bow legs such as chemical disorders in which the long bones of the legs become soft. This means that they will start bending once the child begins to walk, at around one year of age.

Admittedly, a very mild degree of bow leg does occur in perfectly healthy toddlers when they first start walking, but this usually corrects itself with normal growth.

But a significant degree of deformity requires treatment. Obviously, this will include correcting any underlying medical problem, such as rickets. A traditional remedy is to put wedges in the child's shoes in order to try to encourage his legs to grow straight, but this is probably of very limited value. In fact, most severe cases of bow legs have to be corrected by surgery – the surgeon operates on the main bone of the lower leg (the tibia) in order to try to straighten it out.

BREATH-HOLDING ATTACKS

Some small children respond to emotional stress not by having tantrums but by simply gritting their teeth and refusing to breathe. After a minute or so, they become blue in the face and may even lose consciousness; at this stage, normal breathing returns.

This symptom is very alarming for the parents, but they should not seek to startle the child out of his attack by slapping him or splashing him with water. Difficult though it may be to manage, an attitude of calmness and sympathy will give the best results. All children who suffer from breath-holding attacks grow out of them with time.

BRONCHIECTASIS

This is a chronic respiratory condition which is caused by damage to the air passages leading to the lungs. Such damage commonly occurs as a complication of pneumonia, whooping cough or measles.

Typically, bronchiectasis starts in childhood. The boy or girl never really seems to make a good recovery from one or another of the diseases mentioned above, and thereafter is plagued by recurrent coughs which usually keep him or her off school for several months each year.

What has happened is that the damaged air passages have become grossly widened, providing a ready nesting place for germs. Pus collects in these passages and is coughed up in large quantities each morning.

Treatment is a complex business, involving physiotherapy, the use of antibiotics and sometimes lung surgery. Postural drainage of the affected area of lung to drain out all the pus present is of great importance. This means putting your child in whatever position will help to drain the affected patch of lung.

BRONCHIOLITIS

This means inflammation of the smallest air passages leading to the lung. The condition is very common in infants, and is caused by a virus infection. The disorder is more or less the equivalent of acute bronchitis (see *Bronchitis*) in adults or older children. Treatment is similar and, like acute bronchitis, is usually followed by complete recovery.

BRONCHITIS

Yes, children *do* get bronchitis. But it's a totally different condition from the chronic (i.e. long-term) bronchitis of adults. In children, it's an acute (i.e. short-term) condition caused by a virus.

Bronchitis actually means inflammation of the tubes leading to the lungs. In children, it may occur as a complication of colds, 'flu and other virus infections. There is tightness of the chest associated with a dry, painful cough. Later, a good deal of yellow sputum may be produced.

The child should be in a moist atmos-

phere: the use of an old-fashioned steam kettle will help. Failing this, you can get your child to inhale steam from a basin. Depending on the circumstances, the doctor may or may not prescribe antibiotics. In the great majority of cases, the patient is better within a few days.

Alternative therapy
Homoeopathic treatment of bronchitis involves the administration of such agents as aconite, bryonia and belladonna. **Acupuncturists** claim that skilled needling can open up the bronchial passages and make breathing easier. **Naturopaths** and **clinical ecologists** would agree with orthodox doctors that parental cigarette smoke is a potent causative factor and must be avoided at all costs!

BRUCELLOSIS

Now rare in the UK, this is an infection mainly caused by drinking raw milk, which is liable to contain germs. Symptoms include prolonged fever and tiredness.

It's a serious infection, and the diagnosis is difficult to make. So if you go for a holiday in the countryside, don't let your children drink untreated milk!

BRUISES

Most bruises are better left alone without any treatment. There is not the slightest evidence that applying steaks to facial bruises does any good whatever. However, any cold compress will be useful in relieving pain.

Extensive or painful bruising should be treated by a doctor, who will ensure that no more injury is present. He may give an enzyme preparation, such as Chymoral, to hasten absorption of the bruise.

BURNS

See *First Aid*.

CANCER

Thank heavens, cancer is pretty rare in childhood, so it is unlikely that you will have to face the appalling ordeal of having to look after a much loved child with this condition.

However, I have to admit that there are two 'peaks' in cancer during life – a very big one in the later years of our lives, and a small one in childhood (with the years of early adulthood being relatively free of this disease).

Why there should be a 'mini-peak' in childhood is not known. In fact, we haven't the faintest idea of the *cause* of most cases of childhood cancer – though there is some evidence that radiation plays a part in causing at least some cases of leukaemia.

Please bear in mind that the risk of childhood cancer is *very* low: though there are far in excess of 100,000 cases of *adult* cancer per year in Britain, there are only a few hundred childhood cases.

Indeed, the only childhood cancers which most doctors are ever likely to

see are leukaemia, Hodgkin's disease, lymphoma, Wilm's tumour, and neuroblastoma.

Leukaemia is a cancer of the blood, and of the cells which manufacture the blood (see *Leukaemia*).

Hodgkin's disease is a much 'milder' form of cancer (in that the outlook is generally pretty good these days), which affects the child's lymph glands and makes them swell up painlessly. Treatment with anti-cancer drugs such as nitrogen mustard, vincristine or vinblastine plus procarbazine and steroids (cortisone-like drugs) gives very good results indeed. Lymphoma is a very similar condition.

Wilm's tumour (nephroblastoma) is a form of cancer of the child's kidney. The symptom which it produces is that of a rapidly growing abdominal swelling; as soon as the diagnosis is made, the tumour must be removed surgically in order to save the child's life.

Neuroblastoma is a cancer of the child's adrenal gland which is located just above the kidney. Again, the main symptom is a rapidly growing abdominal swelling. Surgical removal, often combined with radiotherapy is the best hope of cure.

CAR SICKNESS

See *Travel sickness*.

CARBON MONOXIDE

POISONING

See *Gas poisoning*, under *First Aid*.

Catarrh

This means the accumulation of mucus in the air spaces behind your child's nose – so that it blocks up the air passages, making it difficult for him to breathe.

Unfortunately, it may get into the tubes which lead from his throat to his ears – making him (at least temporarily) deaf. It increases the chance of ear aches (see *Ear ache*). And it may well drip down into his throat and from there to the tubes leading into his lungs – causing further problems there.

In short, catarrh is a dreadful nuisance. I think that almost every mother must have encountered this problem with her children at some time or another – and lots of kids go on having trouble with it for year after year. Many a parent has been driven nearly to distraction by the endless business of coping with a child whose nose never seems to be free of that infuriating catarrh.

But, luckily for the sanity of parents – in nearly all cases, the catarrh does get better as the child gets older, though he may have little relapses from time to time.

Catarrh forms because of inflammation of the delicate mucous membranes behind the child's nose. These mucous membranes are very sensitive, and when anything irritates them, they're liable to pour out fluid in response to the stimulus.

The sort of things that cause this irritation are air pollutants (especially cigarette smoke), dust, pollen and germs. When children are very young, they are exposed to a barrage of attacks – and their mucous membranes almost invariably respond by producing catarrh. As they get older, children become relatively more resistant to these attacks.

Some children, however, suffer far more from catarrh than others – in others words, they take much longer than others to develop resistance against the assaults that the atmosphere makes on their mucous membranes. No one has discovered why this should be – except that it is known that allergic children do have more trouble with catarrh than other youngsters. This is quite understandable, because dust and pollen in the atmosphere are potent allergy-provokers.

There is, unfortunately, no medicine which makes catarrh go away. All your doctor can do is to give you something to help the symptoms; he can't produce an instant cure. Among the things he's likely to prescribe are·

- Nose drops (often ephedrine), which are helpful if used for a few days – especially if given to a baby half an hour before feeds so that he isn't all snuffly when he's trying to swallow. *Note:* prolonged use of these drops can damage the nose, so your doctor will usually advise giving them for four or five days only, and then throwing the remaining liquid away;

- Inhalants, which are often soothing and comforting to a child. Old-fashioned inhalants can be bought reasonably cheaply over the counter from a chemist and are quite effective for temporary relief of symptoms. So too is inhaling steam if you're stuck and have nothing in the house – but of course, do be careful not to scald the child;

- Antihistamines – these anti-allergy

drugs are of some limited value where there seems to be a definite element of allergy involved in the child's catarrh. However, they don't help the majority and they do have the very marked drawback that they can produce drowsiness;

• Newer anti-allergy inhalers, such as Rynacrom and Beconase. Unfortunately, these are only useful where there is a clear-cut case of allergy to dust or pollen.

There are also other measures you can take to help a child with bad catarrh. First, try cutting down on the irritants to which her nose is exposed, in particular, the dust in her bedroom – especially if she has any degree of dust allergy.

Second, avoid smoking in the house. Cigarette smoke is a very considerable irritant to the nose as well as the chest, and it has now been proved that respiratory troubles are appreciably more common in the children of parents who smoke.

Third, try taking her out in the open air as much as possible, preferably in the countryside. Country air really is very free of pollutants (even today) and even a few hours spent in it gives a child's respiratory passages a rest from the air contaminants which so often provoke bouts of catarrh.

Taking the child swimming regularly can be very good too (unless the chlorine irritates her nose). This is because both the water and the air in swimming pools tend to be fairly free of dust and other pollutants.

One final note: remember that one particular childhood symptom is often due to unsuspected catarrh – and that is night-time cough. If your youngster keeps coughing away in bed, it is most likely that the cause is really undiagnosed catarrh dripping down the back of his throat. See your doctor, who will confirm whether this is so.

Alternative therapy

Homoeopathy treats catarrh with agents such as pulsatilla, nux vomica and potassium iodide. Most alternative therapies quite rightly stress the importance of trying to identify an allergen (e.g. dust, cigarette smoke) and keeping the child away from it. **Clinical ecologists** hold that food allergy (specially to cow's milk and wheat) is an important cause of catarrh.

CEREBRAL PALSY

See *Spastic disorders*.

CHEST DISORDERS

See *Asthma; Bronchiectasis; Bronchiolitis; Bronchitis; Cough; Pleurisy; TB.*

CHICKENPOX

Chickenpox seems to be part of every family's life at some time. Even if your child doesn't actually *get* it, she's bound to come into contact with it at school or playschool.

But although chickenpox is one of the most common of childhood infections, it is also one of the most harmless and trivial. Major complications are rare, which is why there have been no serious efforts to produce a vaccine against it.

There is no cure for chickenpox: antibiotics don't work because it's a virus infection – and drugs like penicillin are ineffective against all viruses. This one circulates in the community all the year round, flaring up in outbreaks every now and again in various parts of the country.

The germ is passed from one child to another in the same way as many other infections – in tiny droplets that are sprayed out during laughing, coughing, sneezing or even just breathing. Children are infectious for a day or two before the rash and a week or so afterwards. It takes about sixteen days to develop – though a child may take between twelve and twenty-one days to come out in spots after exposure. The first indication that something's up is a cry of 'I've got some funny spots, Mummy!' But you may be forewarned if your child has a slight temperature or headache, especially if chickenpox has been going round in your area.

Spots develop on the trunk and on the face (see picture): they're little reddish lumps (A), many of which have blisters of fluid in the centre. The blisters (B) turn into crusts (C) and come off after a few days. Chickenpox spots itch like mad, which is pretty miserable, and it's difficult for a child not to scratch.

If she's small you may find it helpful to put her in light mittens. Keep her nails short and well-trimmed, and make sure that they're clean to reduce the chance of introducing germs into the blisters. Calamine lotion, dabbed on with cotton wool, helps relieve itching. But if that doesn't work try sitting her in a moderately warm bath into which you have put two cupfuls of bicarbonate of soda. Don't give aspirin.

She should stay in bed for a couple of days, but after that she can run about

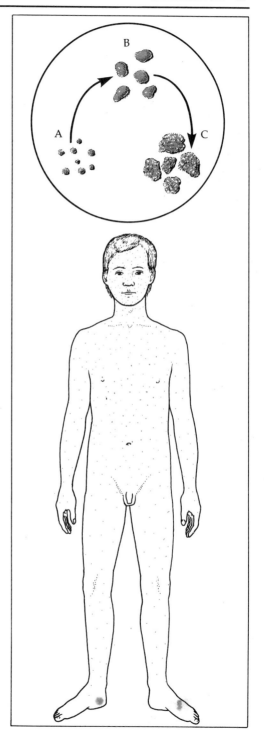

the house or go into the garden. There's usually no need to call the doctor unless you are in doubt about the diagnosis. Don't take your child to your GP's surgery – it just leads to chickenpox being passed to other people.

Your child can play with other children who've already had chickenpox since they'll probably be immune, but she shouldn't go back to playgroup or school until about twelve days after the spots appear. If there are still scabs present give your doctor a ring to check that it's all right to send her back.

Should your child get confused or inexplicably drowsy or has fits while she has chickenpox, contact your GP right away, as these symptoms could indicate that the virus is affecting the nervous system – a very rare complication which needs urgent hospital treatment. (See also *Reye's syndrome*.)

CHILLS

There isn't any such condition as a 'chill'. I know this may be a bit difficult to accept, in view of the fact that the newspapers are always talking about famous people having 'a feverish chill' – but there it is! When people say their child has a chill, they usually mean either a cold (see *Colds*) or 'flu (see *Influenza*).

You may find that grandparents still talk about 'having a chill on a nerve', but again no such condition exists.

CHIROPRACTIC

This is a very interesting form of alternative (complementary) medicine. It's very popular in the USA and is becoming well-known in the UK though there are still only a couple of hundred chiropractors here.

Most people who've had chiropractic would say that it's very like osteopathy (see *Osteopathy*). That's true, because it *is* a form of manipulation. However, chiropractors are very keen on stressing that they're *not* the same as osteopaths. To an 'orthodox' doctor such as myself, there doesn't seem to be all that vast a difference:

But in general: chiropractors go in for 'direct thrusts', rather than the 'long distance leverage' often favoured by osteopaths; and chiropractors say that they use x-rays more than osteopaths do.

Chiropractors, like osteopaths, can be very helpful in treating cases of back pain, and sometimes in other types of joint problem. But I don't feel they'd be useful in other childhood disorders.

In fact, a chiropractor acquaintance of mine tells me that the bulk of their practice is concerned with adults, and that the number of children treated is relatively small.

In the USA and in some other countries, chiropractors do make extraordinary claims for their alleged abilities to treat all sorts of diseases which have nothing to do with the spine or the joints. But this isn't so in Britain, where the small but fast-growing chiropractic profession seems remarkably well organized – and well trained. British chiropractors take a full-time four-year course of college training, after which they're entitled to put the letters DC after their name.

I think it's a measure of their good sense that – unlike certain other alternative practitioners – they don't normally go in for the pretence of calling themselves Doctor.

If you want to find a properly qualified chiropractor for your child, contact:

The British Chiropractors'
    Association
5, First Avenue
Chelmsford
Essex CM1 1RX

CHOLERA

This is a dangerous infection of the intestines, caused by drinking contaminated water. Chief symptom is devastating diarrhoea. It's common in the East, but there have been a few cases in Europe in recent years.

So if you're taking your children to the Orient, or even to the Middle East, ask your doctor about cholera injections well before you go

However, the vaccine *isn't* all that effective. So while you're abroad, take great care not to let your kids drink any water which might possibly be suspect.

CHOREA

This means a type of condition in which there are uncontrollable limb movements.

The kind of chorea which occurs in childhood is called Sydenham's chorea or St Vitus' dance. It's related to rheumatic fever (see *Rheumatic fever*), and is possibly due to an odd reaction to a throat germ. It comes on over a period of several days. Hospitalization is usu-

ally necessary, but most children make a complete recovery.

CIRCUMCISION

Circumcision is the removal of a boy's foreskin (or prepuce), as you can see from the picture below. This operation used to be done very frequently in Britain, but is now quite unusual.

Most parents think of circumcision as a minor operation, but it's important to remember that any operation on a young child carries some risk. Therefore, no operation should be carried out on a baby or toddler unless it's strictly necessary.

Religious circumcision is, of course, different. If you're Jewish and want your newborn son circumcized in the

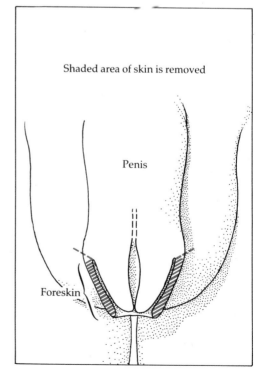

Shaded area of skin is removed

Penis

Foreskin

traditional fashion by the Mohel, then that's fine. (In fact, these specially qualified men are very good at their job, and complications after circumcision performed by them are rare.)

Doctors are far less keen on circumcision for medical reasons than they used to be. Years ago, the great majority of British boys were circumcised soon after birth (that is if their parents could afford it!). After 1948, when the National Health Service was brought in, things began to change. Surgeons were so overloaded with work that they began to look at some of the operations which they had been paid to do, and decide whether they were really needed.

It rapidly became clear that circumcision was nowhere near as much of a necessity as many people had imagined. Indeed, the risk of complications of surgery (including a very occasional death) was so high that many surgeons gradually stopped doing the operation altogether. Today, by my calculations, only about one in every twenty British boy babies is circumcized by a surgeon.

In fact, there *are* a few boy babies who do need circumcision fairly soon after birth. These are the minute number of children whose foreskins are so tight that it is more or less impossible for them to pass water. When they try, the foreskin bulges out like a balloon, because the urine can't get through the very tiny hole in it.

Parents often quite wrongly think that their baby's foreskin is too tight (and assume that he needs circumcision). Like a lot of people – including a few nurses and doctors – they think that the foreskin should 'go back' so as to expose the head (glans) of the penis. However, in a baby this is not neces-

sary. In recent years, surgeons have become more aware of the fact that a baby's foreskin is 'stuck down' to the head of the penis until he's about four or five years old. Until that age, neither you nor anybody else should try to pull it back. So, don't assume that your baby boy needs circumcision just because you can't see the glans of his penis. This is quite normal.

But if you still want your boy circumcized (for reasons other than religion) then talk the matter over with your GP, or with one of the obstetric doctors (the consultant, registrar or house surgeon). If you wish, you can ask for a second opinion from the hospital paediatrician – who, of course, is more expert on babies than an obstetrician would be. You may well find that there is a lot of resistance against doing the operation, and the main reason for this, as I've said, is the possibility of complications – especially accidental injury to the child's penis.

On the plus side, it's true that it's easier for a circumcized male to maintain the hygiene of his penis. Little boys who are not circumcized tend to get a whitish material called smegma collecting under their foreskins. But paediatric opinion these days is that this is no problem, provided that from the age of five or so, boys are taught to pull back the foreskin and wash themselves when they have a bath or shower.

There is also some evidence that little boys who are circumcized at birth do not get cancer of the penis later in life. However, this is a very rare cancer, and is most unlikely to occur in males who wash themselves regularly.

There is also some rather sketchy evidence that if a small boy is circumcized, this may help to protect his future wife against cancer of the cervix, but this is far from proven.

You will neither improve nor harm your baby son's future sex life by having him circumcized. However, it is true that a small proportion of uncircumcized boys find that when they grow up the foreskin won't go back. This is not very good either from a sexual or from a hygienic point of view. These boys can have their problems solved by a circumcision performed during the teenage or adult years, but it's a bit alarming having the operation at this age! The minority of doctors who are still in favour of routine circumcision for all newborn boy babies would say that the procedure is far less traumatic during babyhood than it is in adulthood, and that the baby soon forgets the pain. (The operation is done without an anaesthetic.) But I have a certain sympathy with a surgeon who recently remarked that if you inflicted this sort of pain on a baby for any other reason, you'd be had up for cruelty to children!

CLEFT PALATE AND HARE LIP

To discover that your child has a cleft palate or a hare lip can be a terrible shock. But both conditions can be very successfully treated these days. In fact, the two conditions are closely linked. To understand what cleft palate and hare lip are, let's look at the way in which a baby develops inside the mother's tummy.

In the early days of pregnancy, the head of the foetus is just a rather shapeless blob of tissue. However, as time goes by it begins to take on the semblance and shape of a baby's head. The region of the nose, upper lip and palate is formed by three processes in which tissue grows downward from the area where the eyes are forming. When these three downward projections reach the zone where the mouth will be, they fuse together. The two 'lines of fusion' are roughly in alignment with where the nostrils will form. (See picture, p. 32.)

Sadly, it often happens that something goes wrong with this delicate fusion. If the projections don't join up at the front, then the result will be a hare lip. If they don't join at the back, the baby will have a cleft palate. Very often there is a failure to join at both front and back – the outcome being that the poor baby has both conditions.

Now you can probably see from all this why a hare lip doesn't occur exactly in the middle of the upper lip, like a hare (or a cat). In fact, it occurs slightly to one side, just under the nostril. And if the baby is unlucky, he may have a hare lip on both sides, with just a projection of tissue about a centimetre or so wide under the nose, between the two gaps.

Why do these disasters occur? We don't know. What we do know is that there is occasionally a family tendency to hare lip – though this is not so marked in the case of cleft palate. We also know that these delicate processes by which the various parts of the body are formed during the early weeks of pregnancy are easily disrupted by external factors – for instance, by the mother developing an infection. Another possible external factor is the taking of some drug or medicine.

In fact, so far doctors have not been able to link the development of cleft palate or hare lip to any specific infection, or to any specific tablet or pill, but it does seem common sense for any woman to avoid all medicines and drugs during the first three months of pregnancy if at all possible – and she should take especial care to do so if there is a family history of congenital malformation, such as cleft palate or hare lip. However, there is no reason whatsoever for a woman who gives birth to a baby with one of these two conditions to blame herself.

In the early days of the child's life, there may be problems over feeding, particularly if he has a large cleft in his palate. (Minor degrees of hare lip aren't likely to create much difficulty in sucking.) With care, patience and advice from the midwife, such problems can be overcome. Tube feeding may be necessary in cases of cleft palate.

Doctors don't normally operate on the child right away. The features are very small at this age, and the baby,

being newborn, isn't all that fitted to stand up to extensive operations. But after an interval – sometimes a couple of months, sometimes a good deal longer, depending on the surgeon's preference – the baby's defect will be operated on.

Basically, the operation involves drawing the edges of the gap (or gaps) together, stitching them so that they become attached to each other for life, and carefully refashioning the child's lip.

The results of such operations are remarkable and often leave only the smallest scar so that it is scarcely visible in adult life. The skills of the plastic surgeon can restore almost complete normality to most children. Speech therapy may be necessary after the operation in cases of cleft palate, but it's usually possible to achieve a perfectly good speaking voice.

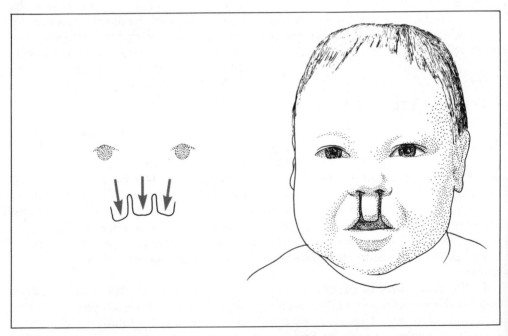

Left: The 3 processes (see p. 31) which grow downwards to form the baby's lip and palate
Right. What happens if the 3 processes don't join together – a double hare lip

To my mind, the development of surgical techniques to deal with these distressing conditions has been one of the great advances of this century.

CLINICAL ECOLOGY

This relatively new alternative therapy has received a lot of publicity in recent years – partly because of the clinical ecologists' belief in such bizarre conditions (or alleged conditions) as 'twentieth century allergy' and 'total allergy syndrome'.

Clinical ecology is a system of medicine which is concerned with proving that many symptoms and illnesses are caused by environmental factors to which the child (or adult) is unusually sensitive.

Clinical ecologists are particularly keen to attribute all sorts of symptoms – psychological and otherwise – to food additives and preservatives, and to cow's milk.

I have to be quite frank and say that at the moment, most doctors are extremely sceptical about the activities of clinical ecologists. Genuine allergists (medical specialists in allergic diseases) regard them as, at worst, quacks – and, at best, as a good excuse for a joke.

On the other hand, two facts have to be admitted:

• today's children (and their parents) *are* exposed to an extraordinary range of chemicals in their food, and in the environment generally;

• certain disorders seem to have become mysteriously more common in recent years – especially allergic conditions like eczema.

It could well be that the increase in these disorders is at least partly linked to the increasing number of chemicals to which we're exposed. Certainly, a few childhood disorders have turned out to be due to abnormal sensitivity to certain agents (for instance, the proteins in wheat and in cow's milk). So there's probably at least an element of common sense in the theory of clinical ecology – even though the wilder claims of its practitioners may be laughable.

In the UK (though not in the USA), most people who call themselves clinical ecologists are qualified doctors. However, it's worth noting that the description clinical ecologist doesn't mean that the doctor in question has any special qualifications as the Press sometimes seem to think. Any doctor (or indeed any person) can award himself/herself the title of clinical ecologist and open a private clinic – which is one reason why orthodox allergy specialists are rather suspicious about this title.

If you decide to take your child to a clinical ecologist, make sure that she or he is medically qualified. Don't spend lots of money without taking your GP's advice about the suggested treatment.

However, please don't let the above note of caution put you off the whole idea of clinical ecology. Quite a few parents – notably those with hyperactive children (see: *Hyperactivity*) – believe firmly that they've been helped by the food exclusion diets recommended by clinical ecologists.

COELIAC DISEASE

Coeliac disease (pronounced 'SEAL-ee-ack') is a moderately common childhood disorder in which an abnormal sensitivity to a certain protein in food prevents the child from absorbing nutrition properly from her intestine. (The word coeliac just means to do with the intestine. The Americans – more sensibly – spell it 'celiac'.)

So, coeliac disease is an intestinal condition, the result of which is recurrent illness and failure to gain weight. Characteristically, the child passes large, pale motions when she goes to the toilet. Wasting of her body may be quite severe, and in years gone by the outlook for such children was appalling, with many of them dying before adulthood.

However, some years ago research demonstrated that coeliac disease is due to an abnormal sensitivity to something called gluten. This is the protein which is found in wheat, rye and barley – and (obviously) in foods which are made from various grains. The abnormal sensitivity is due to a gene, so the condition is inherited. About one in every two thousand children has this disease.

Fortunately, the outlook for these children has been revolutionized by the discovery that the condition is due to sensitivity to gluten. Affected children will now grow strong and healthy provided that their parents keep them on a gluten-free diet.

What are the symptoms of coeliac disease in children? A coeliac baby is absolutely fine while she's on breast milk or bottle milk – because neither human milk nor cow's milk contains any gluten. However, things may start to go wrong after the baby is weaned – because so many of the foods which she is given will be made from wheat, rye and barley.

Therefore, the coeliac baby may well start passing bulky, pale and nasty smelling stools. She may vomit quite a bit, and she may be irritable and lethargic. Very importantly, she may fail to gain weight – but with luck your child health clinic will pick this up.

Some youngsters with coeliac disease may not develop the symptoms until they are much older. In fact, in quite a few people the disease does not develop until adulthood.

Naturally, you shouldn't assume that your baby has coeliac disease just because she has a little diarrhoea or is not putting on weight! The diagnosis can only be made by a doctor. If he suspects that your baby might have coeliac disease, he may refer the baby to a specialist unit for thorough assessments.

If the diagnosis seems a distinct possibility, certain tests will be performed. These include tests on the fat content of the baby's motions. The hospital may also wish to perform a biopsy – a procedure in which a tube is passed down through the baby's mouth in order to obtain a tiny snippet of the lining of the small intestine. When this is examined under the microscope it may show the characteristic damage to the lining of the small intestine which is typical of coeliac disease.

Once gluten is removed from the diet drugs are not really necessary, though in the early stages the child may need antibiotics to combat infection, and perhaps vitamins to make good any deficiencies from which he is suffering. From then on, treatment only consists of making sure that the child keeps to a gluten-free diet.

In general, a coeliac child shouldn't eat any food which contains anything derived from wheat, rye or barley. (There is a possibility that oats might provide gluten as well, but your paediatrician will advise you about this.) In effect, this means that she must steer clear of ordinary bread, buns, rolls, biscuits, cakes and pastry. She will also have to avoid sausages (which contain a good deal of the offending cereals as additives), pasta, packet gravy, semolina and anything cooked in batter. You should also look at the tins and packets of anything you buy, to check that flour is not an ingredient.

While this may sound pretty awful, it is now quite easy to find special bread, biscuits, pasta and flour which do not contain any gluten. Your doctor can give your child a prescription for these, which you take to a baker's just as you would to a chemist. The Coeliac Society (see below) issues a first-class booklet which lists safe food.

Finally, I can't recommend highly enough the work of The Coeliac Society. They are a marvellous self-help group who have done great things for all the many children and adults with coeliac disease in this country. If your child has been diagnosed as a coeliac baby you should write to them, enclosing a large stamped addressed envelope. The address is:

The Coeliac Society
PO Box 181
London NW2 2QY

Alternative therapy
Clinical ecologists agree with orthodox medicine that gluten must be avoided at all costs; some clinical ecologists think that if the child's response is poor, it may be worth excluding soya too.

COLDS

First of all, let's be clear what a cold is. It's an infection of the air passages of the nose – *not* an infection of the chest, as a lot of parents think. So if your child is coughing or wheezy or chesty, she's probably got a chest infection.

Colds are caused by viruses as opposed to bacteria. It is important to understand the difference, because antibiotics (such as penicillin and so on) work on bacteria but they don't work on viruses. Which is why there is no cure for any cold. At the Government Research Station on Salisbury Plain, they've been looking for a cure for colds for thirty years – yet they've found absolutely nothing which will shorten a cold by so much as a single day.

Some parents believe that vitamin C will either make colds better or perhaps keep them away. In fact, the scientists at the Government Research Station – who are to be depended on in such things – believe from their very careful trials that vitamin C doesn't work. But, vitamin C is at least pretty harmless, and side-effects are rare. If you believe in it, then by all means give it to your child, though I wouldn't recommend giving large doses to young babies.

You can, however, give treatment to relieve the symptoms, and make the cold more bearable. The best treatment is usually paracetamol, which you can give to children of a year and upwards. Like many doctors, I dislike those pretty, tasty children's paracetamol – because there is always the danger that a youngster will cheerfully swallow a handful of the nice 'sweeties', or medicine, and do himself in.

In fact, half an adult paracetamol,

once or twice a day, is a perfectly safe treatment for one-year-olds and two-year-olds with a bad cold. But lock the stuff away in the medicine cupboard afterwards! In the case of three- to five-year-olds, you can safely give one adult paracetamol twice a day. He will take it if you crush the tablet up between two teaspoons, and then cover it with his favourite jam.

To relieve a blocked nose, you can get various proprietary inhalations from the chemist. Please follow the instructions very carefully, because damage to the inside of the nose can occur if a child gets too much of some types of inhalant.

A bunged-up nose is a considerable problem in the very young baby, because he may not be able to feed properly. In this case nose drops may be prescribed by your doctor. As these are quite powerful and may damage the nose membranes, your doctor will probably advise you to use them for only about four days – and then to throw them away.

Colds that seem to go on and on probably aren't colds. It could be that your child is getting a cold and then following it up with some other infection, or that he is suffering from an allergy; or chronic catarrh (see *Allergies, Catarrh*).

COLIC

Having had two children who had colic as babies, I'm well aware of how trying this condition can be! This mysterious cause of what seems to be abdominal pain is a real misery for young babies – and for their parents.

Anyone who's spent night after night pacing the bedroom floor with a tiny,

screaming baby will know what I mean. It's impossible to placate the child with this condition – he goes on yelling until you think his lungs must burst! And when he finally seems to have subsided and you crawl thankfully back into bed, it's a fair bet that he'll only wait until you've just dropped off to sleep before beginning all over again. This kind of behaviour has driven many a parent to thoughts of suicide – or murder!

But there is a reasonably bright side to this irritating condition: it always stops in the end. In fact, it's frequently termed three-month colic because by that age it's usually beginning to fade out – though I'm afraid it often lasts longer. But if you're at your wits' end with a baby who screams his head off night after night, you can reflect that in a couple of months' time this misery will almost certainly be over.

Now what causes colic? And why do some babies get it while others don't?

Well, I'm afraid that I have to admit that we don't know.

I'm sure that that will astonish many readers who have been brought up to believe that the condition we call 'colic' is caused by gas trapped inside the baby's intestines or stomach. Why else do we 'burp' little babies? Surely we do it to 'get the wind up' and thereby prevent colic?

This traditional story sounds very plausible, but there is no scientific proof of it at all and these days many paediatricians regard the whole theory as highly unlikely.

Presence of gas inside the intestines will not necessarily produce pain. All of us (babies, children and adults) have large quantities of gas inside us all the time, yet as a general rule this gas produces no pain whatsoever. You can look at the x-rays of hundreds of babies, and you will find that every single one has gas in his or her tummy, even though they are gurgling away happily without a care in the world.

No one ever seems to have undertaken large-scale x-ray studies of babies with colic in order to see if the gas patterns in their insides look any different from those of other babes. I suppose this is because, by and large, babies don't have their attacks of colic at a time when it's easy for doctors to study them. They have them at home, late in the evening or in the middle of the night!

So it may be that the terms 'wind' and 'colic' are completely inappropriate for this mysterious condition. In my own mind, I prefer to think of it as 'babyhood night-time screaming' (which emphasizes that most of the time we haven't the faintest idea what the baby is screaming about!). But for the sake of convenience, I'm going to continue here to refer to the disorder as colic.

Incidentally, it's interesting that this colic does seem to be a good deal more common in Western civilization than in less developed countries. Several years back, the distinguished paediatrician Dr Hugh Jolly (speaking on 'The Jimmy Young Show') expressed his puzzlement at the cause of these attacks and pointed out that in some Third World countries they are quite unknown. In many parts of the globe, he told listeners, mothers would be completely baffled if they saw you trying to burp a baby and would wonder what on earth you were doing! Indeed, this was my own experience when I worked in the West Indies some years ago.

To sum up, the syndrome we call colic is characterized by night-time screaming attacks starting not long after birth and usually finishing by the age of three to six months. Something is obviously upsetting the baby and making it scream, but we don't really know what.

It might be useful to ask yourself the following questions when a baby is drawing up his legs and screaming:

1 Is he actually ill? Though a serious illness is a very uncommon cause of screaming attacks, you should of course bear this in mind. If a baby's screaming is accompanied by diarrhoea or the passing of bloodstained stools, or if he has a temperature of over 37·8°C (100°F) taken in the armpit, then telephone your doctor.

2 Has he swallowed a lot of air? Although, as I've said, the relationship between air in the tummy and screaming attacks is quite unproven, it certainly does sometimes happen that a child's crying stops after a big burp (though admittedly it might be out of sheer surprise). If this is the case with your baby, ask yourself why he may be swallowing too much air. It could, for instance, be that there is some simple problem with his bottle (say, too small a hole in the teat) and your health visitor could help you sort this out.

3 Does his feed disagree with him? Unsuitable food certainly can upset babies' tummies. A point to bear in mind is that quite a few babies are actually allergic to cow's milk (something few doctors realized until relatively recently). All baby milks are, of course, made from cow's milk, even though some of them have been modified in order to give them a reasonable resemblance to mother's milk in chemical constitution.

Even if your baby isn't allergic to cow's milk, it could well be that the way the feed is being made up is upsetting him. Surveys have shown that a large percentage of parents do make quite enormous mistakes while making up their babies' feeds. So if your baby is bottle-fed and is having colic, you should get your health visitor to watch you prepare a bottle and tell you if you're doing anything wrong.

4   Is the feeding technique wrong? It's also very easy to make mistakes, and here again your health visitor can help to sort out little problems. Difficulties with technique are less common with breast-feeding than with bottle-feeding, and this may be part of the reason why colic seems to me to be rather less commonly encountered in breast-fed babies – though of course some of them do get it. (Bear in mind too what we said about cow's milk allergy – no baby is going to be allergic to his mother's milk.)

5   Is the baby hungry and just plain uncomfortable? This is perhaps rather an unlikely one, since most mothers make jolly sure that a screaming baby is well fed and as comfortable as possible. But occasionally it does turn out that an attack of screaming has been triggered off because the child has a rampaging thirst, or has a pin digging in him, or is being chafed by his nappy.

6   Is the baby being made tense and upset by the way he's handled? Strange as it may sound, this factor is now very strongly favoured by paediatricians as a possible trigger of colic. So often, it turns out that the child starts his screaming attack after a rather hurried evening feed when Mum is rushing to get things ready for Dad's arrival home. It's almost as if he feels that he's being neglected or rushed. And oddly enough, babies do seem to have an extraordinary ability to sense tension in their mothers. Again and again, the woman who is anxious and on edge when handling her new baby finds that the child develops colicky screaming attacks – which in turn make poor Mum feel even worse. It's a vicious circle. (Of course, a colicky child inevitably makes a mother upset – it's all too easy for a doctor to blame the child's symptoms on the mother's tension – not realizing that it may really be the other way round!)

Consult your Health Visitor and, if necessary, your GP or Child Health Clinic about the problem. Your doctor may possibly decide to prescribe a little anti-colic or mildly sedative medicine for the baby, though some paediatricians feel that the only good such preparations do is to reassure the child's parents.

Alternative therapy

This may be well worth trying, in a condition in which orthodox doctors are so unsuccessful! **Homoeopaths** have a whole battery of anti-colic remedies. **Clinical ecologists** say that 'almost invariably' the cause is sensitivity to cow's milk or its products. If a breast-fed child develops colic, then they say that her *mother* should avoid cow's milk and milk products.

COLITIS *(ulcerative)*

See *Ulcerative colitis*.

COLOUR BLINDNESS

This condition occurs in various forms. Far and away the most frequently encountered is the type in which red and green are confused. This is an inherited condition, present in about 3 per cent of all boys, but not in girls. Affected people often don't realize that they have the defect, which obviously troubles them very little, except if they are working in jobs which require accurate colour differentiation.

COMA

For care of a child who is in coma see *Unconsciousness* under *First Aid*.

COMPLEMENTARY MEDICINE

See *Alternative medicine*.

CONCUSSION

Concussion is surprisingly common in children who've had a blow to the head. The belief, engendered by countless films and novels, that a human being can usually take a severe blow to the head with little or no effect (beyond a few minutes of unconsciousness) is dangerous nonsense.

Anyone who is struck by a violent blow on the skull probably sustains some brain injury, however minor. If slight confusion or even the shortest period of unconsciousness follows, the child must go to hospital and have a full examination and an x-ray.

In many hospitals, it's the invariable practice to admit any youngster who has been knocked out for a night's observation. Even so, a considerable number of patients with apparently trivial head injuries, who have not even been KOd, still die each year because of undetectable brain damage.

You should, therefore, always act with extreme caution. If your child is struck on the head, observe her carefully over the next twenty-four to forty-eight hours. Contact a doctor or take her to an accident and emergency department if she becomes unusually drowsy, or confused or starts vomiting.

CONGENITAL DISLOCATION OF THE HIP

Congenital dislocation of the hip (CDH) is quite common. In the old days, it crippled many children. These days – provided that the disorder is detected early enough, and treated – this shouldn't happen.

When a newborn baby leaves hospital, he should have had a routine 'medical' carried out by one of the doctors. (I say should because, as you probably know, the NHS is rather desperately overstretched these days. If your baby doesn't seem to have had such a medical, then ask for one to be carried out!)

If CDH isn't noticed before the baby leaves hospital, there's a good chance that the problem will be picked up at your child health clinic. And once the disorder is diagnosed, it can be cured.

A normal hip joint in a baby consists of a sort of ball and socket joint – with the head of the thighbone forming the ball. This fits into the socket – which is the little cup in the pelvic bone.

When a baby is suffering from CDH,

the ball at the top of the thighbone isn't firmly in the cup of the socket because the socket is too shallow. So sometimes the ball is inside the cup – but at the drop of a hat, it'll slip out!

The reason why this development abnormality occurs in so many children – girls more than boys – isn't known, though it might be due to increased pressure inside the womb.

At her first routine medical your baby should be given one or two special tests called the Ortolani test and Barlow's test. They both involve moving the hip joint to see if there is a distinct click or clunk as the head of the thighbone slips out of the socket. (See picture below.)

If the doctor suspects that the condition is present, an x-ray is taken to try and confirm the diagnosis. However, lots of babies have clicking hips – but don't actually have CDH. The reason why their hips click isn't known, and usually all that happens is that they are followed up by the hospital until the click eventually vanishes.

There are basically two kinds of treatment for CDH: non-surgical and surgical.

Non-surgical treatment is always used if the problem is picked up early enough. This involves holding the child's thigh bones wide apart with some sort of splint over a period of many months – so that the head of the thigh bone will eventually become firmly settled into the socket. Newborn babies are generally put into a padded splint, shaped like an X or an H – and they remain in it for up to six months.

Larger babies may go into a metal frame, which is usually followed up by a plaster splint on both legs – the so-called 'frog' plaster. This has a 'gap' so that the

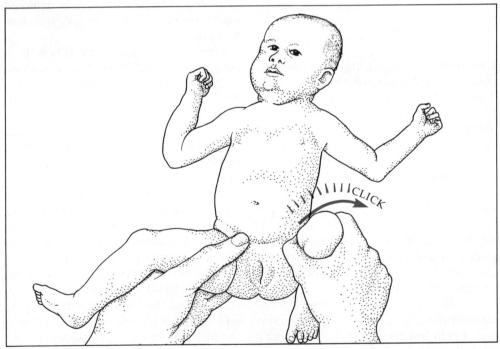

All babies should be checked by a doctor for the 'click'

baby can go to the loo. With girls in particular, it may be difficult to keep urine from making the plaster wet and soggy – unfortunately, this may cause chafing. Protection of the skin with Vaseline or a barrier cream may help, but take your health visitor's advice. If the plaster crumbles or frays badly around the crotch, get the hospital to repair or replace it before it can chafe the baby badly.

Surgery is only used when CDH isn't diagnosed until later on in childhood – or in the rare cases where splinting the legs has failed. There are various operations, but a typical one is the 'shelf operation', in which a small wedge of bone is taken out of the pelvic bone and inserted on the edge of the socket, so as to keep the head of the thigh bone from popping out.

The results of surgery are pretty good these days, but it is obviously better if CDH can be diagnosed as early as possible. So, all parents should make sure that their babies do have that routine medical early in life.

CONJUNCTIVITIS

This word means inflammation of the conjunctiva (pronounced conn-junk-TIE-vah). This is the thin, transparent membrane which covers the white of your child's eye. But conjunctiva isn't intimately concerned with vision. So inflammation is unlikely to affect your child's sight, and wildly unlikely to make him blind.

That's why this very common condition isn't usually at all serious (though in newborn babies, it must be promptly treated – see below).

The classic symptoms of conjunctivitis are:
- pinkness or redness of the child's eye;
- a yellow discharge – which is specially noticeable in the mornings, when it has usually solidified;
- an uncomfortable feeling in the eye;
- sometimes, redness and puffiness of the eyelids.

Of course, we've all had very mild conjunctivitis at some time or other – perhaps woken up with a very slightly pink eye and a trace of yellow material ('sleep') in the corner. What has happened is that some slight irritation (perhaps caused by a speck of dust) has inflamed the conjunctiva.

However, *germs* can also cause inflammation of the conjunctiva – and in young children this can be quite unpleasant. If certain nasty little bugs get into a child's eye, they can produce a more severe conjunctivitis, with intense swelling of the lids and a really profuse discharge.

If your child gets this, you should of course take him to the doctor at the next available surgery, so that some antibiotic eye ointment and/or drops can be prescribed. (Your doctor may wish to take a swab first, and send it to the lab.)

If you have to wait a day or two before you can see your GP (perhaps because it's the weekend), all you need to do in the meantime is to bathe the child's eye two or three times a day with Optrex. But do remember that his eye (and the pus from it) is infectious. This means that you should wash your hands very thoroughly after bathing the eye and wash the eyebath out very carefully with hot soapy water, too.

If infection of the conjunctiva occurs in the newborn, it's potentially more serious, and always needs very prompt treatment because the germs which attack this age group can be quite harmful. But commonly it occurs when you and your baby are still in hospital so that this prompt treatment is almost invariably supplied. A swab is taken, and antibiotic ointment prescribed.

And if you're at home, a good rule is that any baby under a year who has conjunctivitis needs fast treatment. In all circumstances, the child should be seen by a doctor within about twelve hours so that an antibiotic ointment or drops can be prescribed. Meanwhile just wipe the baby's eyes from time to time with balls of cotton wool dipped in tepid water. Use a separate piece for each eye, and immediately throw the used pieces away. Wash your hands at once after touching the baby's eyes.

Many parents find putting drops into the child's eyes a major stumbling-block. The trick is to get round behind him and do it from above his head. A toddler or older child will usually sit in a chair with his head tilted back while you stand behind him and put the drops or ointment in. A baby, on the other hand, is best wrapped in a blanket and held firmly on a bed by someone else while you do the necessary.

When putting in drops hold the child's upper eyelid open with one hand; with the other, aim the dropper somewhere near the side of his eyeball which is nearer his nose. Let him have a blink after each drop. To insert ointment, just hold down the lower lid and firmly squirt about half an inch of the stuff along the inner side of the lid.

Remember to throw away both ointment and drops at the end of the course. If kept for another time the medicine may be contaminated.

CONSTIPATION

This means an inability to pass bowel motions as often as desired. Unfortunately, that's a very relative expression. In other words, if you think your child should have his bowels open every day, then you're going to regard a three-times-a-week bowel action as constipation. If you couldn't care less how often your youngster has his bowels open, then you won't regard three times a week (or even once a week) as being constipation. If you take the view that it doesn't matter to his health, you'd be right.

Very regrettably, parents who worry about their own bowels nearly always worry about their children's toilet performance too. They may start giving the youngsters laxative drugs, or they may keep taking them down to the GP, with a plaintive cry of 'He's always constipated, doctor'.

If you don't worry about your bowels – or your children's bowels – you don't need this entry: turn the page and forget it. I'm with you: I've never taken the least interest in whether my sprogs have been to the loo or not, and they don't seem any the worse for it.

However, I do appreciate that there are a lot of parents who are very concerned about bowel habits. It's easy for doctors to poke fun at them for being pernickety and obsessive, but if you've been brought up to think that once-a-day regularity and so-called inner cleanliness is of great importance, then it's very hard to free yourself of the attitudes of a lifetime. In fact, if your Mum or Dad went on at you about regularity then it's very difficult for you not to do the same to your own kids.

Mothers and fathers who worry about whether their kiddies have 'been' or not may not always get a great deal of help from today's doctors. It's true that doctors used to believe that there was a serious illness called constipation and that it made you ill if you didn't quickly take something to clear all the nasty stuff out of your system.

But today most doctors think that that's a load of old malarkey. They believe that the ancient idea that everyone should 'go' once a day is quite wrong. They recognize that some kids (and adults) go two or three times a day – while others only go once a week! The latter, I should add, are in perfect health and don't suffer from headaches or 'absorption of poisons' or any of the other things that were supposed to happen if you didn't have a good daily clear-out.

Well, if you are a bowel-conscious parent, what should you do? First, don't let your anxiety about regular bowel function transmit itself to your children. If you do, then as sure as fate you will find that very early in their little lives they will set about thwarting you – by deliberately hanging on to their bowel motions. Since they're usually as stubborn as you, the stage is set for a great old battle which may continue for years!

Don't give the poor child drugs – and by drugs I mean laxatives, aperients, opening medicines – call them what you will. In recent years, it's been recognized that giving people regular doses of these potions (which were once considered so essential to the well-being of every child and adult) eventually conditions the bowel to expect them. The result is bowel trouble where none existed before – quite the reverse of what the poor parents intended when they started giving out doses of syrup of figs or Andrew's Liver Salts!

If you find it hard to accept that children should be allowed to 'go' as and when they want to – not on rigidly laid-down schedule – then instead of laxatives, just give your family lots of fruit and vegetables.

Fruit and veg are full of fibre – which stimulates the bowel to work naturally. So too is bran, but don't get too carried away with the current fashion: if you give really massive doses of the stuff, you can actually produce a blockage of the bowels!

Finally, try to ignore the persistent urgings of others who say: 'But it's not right, dear: he hasn't been today.' He'll survive!

Alternative therapy

Homoeopaths tend to treat constipation with bryony and a light roughage diet, which is fair enough. Like **naturopaths**, they often blame aluminium in saucepans for constipation, and advise the parents to change to stainless steel or enamel.

CONVULSIONS

See *Epilepsy*, and also *Feverish convulsions*.

COUGH

A cough is obviously one of the most common of all symptoms – both in children and in adults. All youngsters get a cough from time to time. Here are the likely causes:

- chest infections (see *Chest Disorders* for a list of these)

- catarrh
- colds in which there is a lot of muck dripping down the back of the throat
- 'croupy' coughs
- asthma
- tonsillitis – though other symptoms are usually more striking
- whooping cough

Rarer and more serious causes include inhaled foreign bodies (which require emergency first aid), and tuberculosis (see *TB*).

A child coughs because there's something irritating his air passages. It may be anywhere from the back of the throat down to the lungs, but that irritation sends a message up the nerves which lead to the cough centre in the brain.

The message (roughly decoded) says "Ere, cough centre – we've got some trouble down below in the pipes. Give a good cough and see if you can't get rid of it.'

So the cough centre sends an order down to the muscles of your child's chest, telling them to make him cough. The cough may be distressing for him, but it may well dislodge some of the irritation in the air passages.

So, very often it's a good idea for a child to cough, because it gets all the 'yuk' out of his chest or throat. I know that children don't usually spit it out like adults do – instead they usually swallow it! But at least it's out of their lungs, where it can do most harm.

Deciding the cause of the cough (which usually falls into one of the seven categories mentioned above) is up to your doctor. Most mild coughs don't need his attentions, but in the case of a severe cough (one which is really distressing to the child) or one that goes on for a week or more, the youngster ought to be examined.

Treatment of all these possible causes of cough is discussed in all the relevant entries.

Very often parents want treatment in the form of cough medicine. Suppressing the cough with medicine is often quite easy – but, do bear in mind that this may not be a good thing at all, and that a cough is usually a way of getting rid of dangerous phlegm.

Alternative therapy
Homoeopaths often use drosera or bryonia to treat coughs. **Clinical ecologists** would look for an inhaled agent to which the child is sensitive, or a food allergy.

CROHN'S DISEASE

Pronounced 'Crone's', this is a condition which is quite common in adults but fairly rare in children. It's an inflammation of the intestine, which produces symptoms such as abdominal pain, diarrhoea and sometimes rectal bleeding. Unfortunately, the cause isn't known. Drugs and surgery can be helpful.

Parents of children with Crohn's disease should contact:

Crohn's in Childhood Research
56A Uxbridge Road
Shepherd's Bush
London W12

CROUP

This word describes the strange noise which a sick child (particularly one with a throat or chest infection) produces as he breathes. It is produced by narrowing of the child's air passages – so parents should always regard croup as an important symptom, and let the doctor know about it.

People tend to talk about 'a baby suffering from croup' as though it were a disease in itself. It isn't; it's just a symptom.

All the air we breathe has to flow through the voicebox, which is located in the throat, at the level of the Adam's apple. Even in adults, the opening is very narrow indeed; in an infant, it's scarcely wide enough to admit a pencil.

So it's easy to see that a child's airway can very readily become blocked. And when this obstruction occurs (whatever the cause) the result is the crowing sound we call croup.

What can cause this blockage? Well, first an inhaled or half-swallowed foreign body can do it I vividly remember an occasion during a holiday in one of the wilder parts of the Outer Hebrides (far from any hospital) when my baby son suddenly started to crow. Moments later, as the degree of obstruction increased, he began to turn an ominous shade of dark blue.

The croup was of such sudden onset that I felt certain it was due to some small object lodged in his throat, so I applied the standard first aid treatment, which is to hold the baby upside down by his ankles and smack him sharply between the shoulder blades.

This didn't help at all. Things were looking very sinister now, because the croupy noise had suddenly stopped, though the baby's chest was heaving desperately. No air was coming in or out – the obstruction was complete.

There's no doubt that the baby could have been dead within a minute or two. Fortunately, by running my forefinger back over his tongue I was just able to hook my nail round the object that was jammed in his throat – a piece of toy roof tile. As it came out, there was a great rush of air into his chest, and within seconds, his colour had changed from near-black to a good, healthy pink. He made a rapid and complete recovery.

But in the majority of cases of croup, the obstruction is caused not by a foreign body but by some form of inflammation of the larynx – laryngitis, in fact.

The commonest kind of laryngitis in an infant is often called spasmodic croup. The child, who has usually (though not always) had a slight head cold for a day or so, suddenly develops a bout of coughing and becomes quite hoarse. Within a few minutes he's making the kind of croupy noise I've described, though fortunately his colour remains good.

In the case of this or any other kind of croup, always contact the doctor.

A few doctors find it may be useful if you can let the child breathe near the phone, so that she can make some assessment of the urgency of the condition simply by listening.

Until medical help arrives, the best emergency treatment is to get the child into a very moist atmosphere. The old-fashioned steam kettle was ideal for this purpose, but you can help the child's breathing simply by carrying him into the kitchen and holding him near the jet of steam from the spout of an ordinary kettle (but not, of course, too near). Sitting him in the bathroom close by a steaming shower is also effective.

Another (and much more dangerous) type of croup is the kind you get with an infection called laryngo-tracheo-bronchitis. This mouthful of a name means that there is severe inflammation of the voicebox, the windpipe and the main tubes of the lungs. The child has usually had a chesty cough and a temperature for a few hours; suddenly, his breathing becomes very tight and he starts to crow.

If his face starts to turn blue, there's no time to lose. In these circumstances, it's usually best to take him to the nearest casualty department, especially if your own doctor cannot be contacted immediately. If breathing stops on the way to the hospital, try to give him the kiss of life.

Diphtheria also causes laryngitis and hence croup, but this disease is now so rare that you can forget all about it – provided you've had your child immunized. If you haven't, then I suggest you make the arrangements with your doctor right away.

Whooping cough too is also a cause of a croupy noise, and in this disease, it occurs as the infant sucks in air after a bout of ten or a dozen spasmodic coughs. Again, put the child into a very moist atmosphere, and always contact the doctor right away for further advice.

Fortunately, most kids with croup come through it but don't mess around with this alarming symptom. Ring the doctor immediately and ask her advice.

CUTS

See *First Aid*.

CYSTIC FIBROSIS

Cystic fibrosis (or fibrocystic disease) is a relatively uncommon condition which occurs about once in every 2000 babies, and which causes a very great deal of distress. One in 20 adults is a hidden carrier of the gene.

Also known as CF or mucoviscidosis, it's a disease in which the mucus produced by certain organs of the body is far thicker and more viscid than normal. The affected organs may include the child's lungs and pancreas.

Because CF is due to inheritance of a faulty gene, there's sometimes a history of another affected child in the family. This may help to give a clue to the diagnosis – which is not always easy.

The disease tends to show itself in one of three ways:

- recurrent chest infections. The production of thick mucus in the lungs may give the baby or toddler recurring and severe bouts of coughing and wheezing;
- blockage of the intestines in the newborn. This occurs because the disease has hit the pancreas – which therefore cannot produce the juices which should digest food;
- frequent passing of large, pale bowel motions. This again is due to disease of the pancreas.

The diagnosis of CF is made by finding unusually high amounts of salt in the child's sweat (mothers often notice that the child tastes abnormally salty).

This is a very serious disease. But the outlook has improved quite a bit in recent years. Treatment may include antibiotics to control lung infections, aerosol inhalations, drugs to thin thick mucus, drugs to open up the air passages, oxygen, physiotherapy, vitamin supplements, and a digestion-promoting powder called pancreatin which helps replace the missing pancreatic juices.

A system of breathing called FET (Forced Expiration Technique) is taught by physios and is of great help to children who are old enough to learn it.

If you're the parent of a CF child, you should most certainly join the excellent self-help organization:

The Cystic Fibrosis Research Trust
5 Blyth Road
Bromley
Kent BR1 3RS

Cystitis

See *Urinary problems*.

Dandruff

Quite a lot of children get dandruff, which can be a source of considerable embarrassment and irritation to them – especially if other people remark on it.

It's not, as parents often imagine, spread from child to child by combs – in fact, it's not caused by germs, and is therefore completely non-infectious. It is related to an over-dryness of the scalp, with consequent scaling of the top layer of skin (seborrhoea).

Mild dandruff can usually be kept in check by the regular use of a proprietary 'medicated' shampoo. The word medicated usually indicates that the preparation contains aspirin in liquid form.

Some anti-dandruff shampoos contain an antiseptic, though the value of this is doubtful, since, as already mentioned, the condition is not caused by germs.

More severe dandruff needs treating by a GP, or sometimes by a dermatologist. Difficult cases may never clear up entirely, but can usually be kept well under control. When dandruff appears in adolescence, there is a tendency to natural improvement, and many patients lose the condition completely by the time they are adults.

Deafness

If you ever suspect your child may be even slightly deaf, you should have her hearing checked out.

If deafness isn't diagnosed promptly (and appropriate action taken), it's almost certain that great harm will be done to a child's educational, social and emotional development.

Unfortunately, it still quite often happens that a baby is *not* diagnosed as being wholly or partly deaf. And by the time anybody finds out, she'll have dropped far behind other children in acquiring linguistic and other skills. You can imagine the damage that this may cause her.

In fact, deafness ought to be picked up on routine hearing checks at child health clinics – and in many cases, it is. Treatment and/or special help with speech can then be started.

There are many possible causes of childhood deafness, including German measles during pregnancy, meningitis and recurrent ear infections. Sadly, I have to admit that in many cases we don't know why a child is born deaf.

Temporary deafness may accompany ear ache (see *Ear ache* for further information).

Being the parent of a deaf child can be very difficult indeed – but it can also be quite extraordinarily rewarding, if you can manage to help the child to cope with this severe handicap.

DEPRESSION

Yes, depression does occur in children – particularly older ones – though nowhere near as frequently as it does in adults. Fortunately, really severe depression (for instance, involving a genuine suicidal attempt) is quite rare.

But a child's complaint of being 'depressed' should always be treated seriously, since it's probably quite genuine. Apart from just feeling miserable, other possible symptoms include severe insomnia, loss of appetite and 'playing hookey' from school.

Obviously, you should try and find out why your child is depressed – it may be related to bullying at school, or to trouble between Mum and Dad. Don't hesitate to ask your doctor about the possibility of referral for specialist help.

DERMATITIS

See *Eczema*.

DIABETES

Diabetes is quite common in childhood – and used to be a death sentence for most of the children who got it. That appalling situation was changed one day in Toronto in 1921 when two young Canadian researchers called Frederick Banting and Charles Best managed to save a diabetic boy's life with the revolutionary new treatment of injections of insulin – a hormone extracted from the pancreas gland of animals.

From that time forward, it has been possible for all children with diabetes to survive, and to live normal, healthy lives.

Despite the commonness of this disease, I find that very few parents have any real notion of what the word diabetic means when they are first told that their child is suffering from the condition.

The human body runs on fuel – and that fuel is glucose. Glucose is, if you like, the petrol on which human beings run. Now your first reaction may be to say 'Yes, but I don't very often eat glucose'. However, the fact is that a great deal of the food which you eat is broken down into glucose by your digestive system, so that it can be used by your body as fuel.

In the same way as cars won't work unless there is a spark of electricity to help burn the petrol, the body's glucose can't be burned unless there is something to help it burn – and that something else is called insulin.

You have plenty of insulin in your body. It's a chemical produced by your pancreas – a gland located near your stomach. (You'll find them among the rather grotty-looking group of glands described by the butcher as 'sweetbreads'.)

In diabetic children, something goes badly wrong with the pancreas. We still don't really understand why – but the result is that not enough insulin is produced to burn up the body's glucose. If there is insufficient insulin produced, the level of glucose in the body starts to rise in a rather sinister manner.

Soon there is so much glucose in the body that the only way that the diabetic child can get rid of it is by passing it out in the urine. And that is why one of the most important warning signs of diabetes is a tendency to pass very large quantities of urine.

Other prominent symptoms are extreme thirst and marked weight loss. Some children also get a lot of boils, probably because the germs which cause boils thrive in the sugary environment which is associated with a high blood glucose.

So any child who has any of the above symptoms should certainly be taken to his GP, who will test the urine for glucose. If the test is positive, this is a strong indication of the presence of diabetes – though further investigation will probably be necessary to confirm the diagnosis.

If your child has got diabetes, it's bound to come as a shock. You may not even be able to take all of it in to begin with.

But take courage: things are nowhere near as bad as they might seem. The modern treatment of diabetes is so successful that virtually all children who have it will none the less grow up to be pretty healthy adults.

However, as diabetes isn't normally a curable condition, both parents and child have to realize that if a youngster is to avoid becoming seriously ill, he must stick to his treatment throughout his entire life.

The most important part of the treatment is diet and insulin injections.

(Many adult diabetics are treated with tablets – or simply with diet alone – instead of insulin injections. But since this is rare in childhood diabetes, except in certain ethnic groups – including West Indians – I don't propose to deal with this type of treatment here.)

I've put diet before insulin because many people seem to think that the treatment of diabetes just consists of having insulin jabs. That's quite untrue.

A diabetic child's diet will unfortunately have to be strictly controlled from now on. He should have no added sugar – and no sweets or chocolate. And he'll have to stick to a diet plan, prepared by the hospital, which regulates the amount of starchy things (like bread, potatoes, biscuits and so on) which he can eat. In the last few years, hospitals have quite rightly taken to emphasizing the importance of healthy fibre-containing vegetables and fruit in a diabetic child's diet. And it's very important to stress that most hospital clinics don't restrict protein foods like meat, fish and cheese, and the fatty foods like butter, margarine and cooking oil. But on general health grounds, polyunsaturated fats are probably better than saturated ones.

In short, it's perfectly possible for the child to have school lunches, and to eat his meals with his family. All he has to do is to ration himself according to his diet sheet as far as potatoes, bread and other starchy foods are concerned. This may sound difficult to an adult but it's quite astonishing how quickly a child learns to do it!

Incidentally, there is no need for the youngster's food to be weighed at every meal. After a few weeks, most children learn to judge by eye whether they've got about four or about six ounces of spuds on their dinner plate. (In fact, they're mostly learning to do it in grams these days.) There's certainly no need to cart a pair of scales to school!

In practice, a diabetic child's diet is usually pretty generous, and few of them complain about anything other than the loss of their sweets.

The diabetic child must also have his insulin injections as prescribed by the doctor in charge of his case. This is vital, because if he doesn't get his insulin injections he will slowly lapse into a coma and die.

The type of insulin, the quantity and the precise time at which it should be given are all prescribed by the specialist. It is quite amazing how young diabetic children very rapidly learn to measure out their dose of insulin in the syringe, and give themselves the jab. In many ways, they're a lot braver than we are!

The other thing which the youngster should learn to do for himself is to test his own urine for glucose, and to record the amount found at each test in a small notebook, which should be taken to the GP or to the hospital doctor at every visit. In this way, he and his parents should have an early warning of any tendency for his diabetes to go out of control.

The newer method of blood (rather than urine) testing gives even better control. In fact it is by far the best way of ensuring that the child's diabetes remains in balance – without either too much glucose, or too little.

Sensible parents can reduce a child's insulin slightly if his urine tests show that his glucose is always low and if he keeps getting the low-glucose reactions called 'hypos', in which he becomes confused or may even possibly have a fit.

And if the urine or blood tests show that his glucose is too high, they will increase his insulin slightly.

In short, balance is everything in diabetes. It's not surprising that the motto of the British Diabetic Association is 'Balance is Life'.

The parents of any diabetic child will find it well worth while to join the Association for all the help and information that it gives. The address to write to is:

British Diabetic Association
10 Queen Anne Street
London W1

Alternative therapy

Alternative remedies really aren't a great idea in a condition like diabetes, where the child's life depends on adhering strictly to orthodox medical treatment. However, I'll just add that **clinical ecologists** claim that 'a large percentage' of diabetics have low chromium levels, and that their diabetes will become much milder if they are given 'enormous oral doses of chromium'. Though this treatment *may* be harmless, I think you should talk it over carefully with your doctor before letting your child have it.

DIARRHOEA

Alas, every parent is all too familiar with the fact that children do tend to have diarrhoea at times – and often in the most wildly inconvenient and embarrassing places (like in aeroplanes, or half way up the motorway!). Let's look at the possible causes.

Diarrhoea in young babies is a common symptom, and often one of little significance, but if it persists it is best dealt with by the family doctor or health clinic. Many babies have a loose bowel action after every feed, and continue to do so for the first six months of life. In others, diarrhoea is simply a reaction to too much sugar in the feed. In a very small proportion of children, it may indicate some important underlying disorder such as coeliac disease (see *Coeliac disease*).

Diarrhoea in older babies, toddlers or children can occasionally be due to cystic fibrosis (see *Cystic fibrosis*) or other serious conditions, but is far more likely to be part of the infectious diarrhoea and vomiting (D&V) that affects nearly all families at some time or other.

Very often, several of the family get it at once, or one after the other. And often it's the young children who suffer most. This is because the fluid loss caused by an attack of D&V can be very much more serious for a tiny child, whose fluid reserves are much smaller than those of a grown-up. An attack in a young baby can have devastating consequences, since severely dehydrated (that is, fluid-lacking) babies can die with alarming speed. Admittedly, most bouts of D&V are *not* serious – but never regard diarrhoea or vomiting in a baby as something trivial. If you're in any real doubt, you should ring your doctor and ask his advice.

Some parents still seem to think that diarrhoea and vomiting is some kind of 'act of God' – in other words, that it just happens by some strange mischance. In fact, most cases of D&V are caused by infection – with little bugs which are all too readily spread from one human being to another. That's why D&V so often spreads through a family.

It starts with someone who is excreting the bugs in his or her bowel motions, and who may or may not feel ill. If a germ from this person's bowel motions gets into someone else's food or drink, then – bingo! – down they go with the squitters, unless they're lucky enough to have resistance to this particular germ.

But young children – unlike adults – don't often have resistance to such bugs, because they haven't been exposed to them before.

You may wonder how germs from one person's bowel motions can contaminate another person's food. In fact, it's the easiest thing in the world for this to happen.

It's the ease of transmission by this bowel-to-mouth route that has caused the great epidemics of cholera and typhoid that have swept the world for centuries. The same is true of plain, ordinary D&V. It will, for instance, be transmitted if someone in the family fails to wash their hands thoroughly after wiping their bottom. Five minutes later, that person lays a hand on baby's bottle or baby's rusks – or even sticks a finger in baby's mouth – and ker-pow! baby gets the germ – and is therefore in for a very nasty bout of D&V.

Also, it requires only a touch of the nose while cooking (something many people do without even realizing it) to transfer nose germs to your family's food.

Here are a few basic rules for prevention of D&V in the home. It's impossible to rule out all attacks, but you can cut the chances of it occurring to a minimum by following these principles:

- make sure that all members of your family wash their hands after passing a bowel motion (washing after having a pee isn't particularly important).
- try to get your family to wash their

hands before meals – a quick rinse is sufficient.

- ensure that anyone who is preparing food – or babies' bottles – has washed their hands first.
- don't leave still-frozen chickens out in your kitchen, where the germs which are present in them can contaminate other food.
- don't let anyone who has boils on their hands, or a septic finger, prepare food or babies' bottles.
- breast-feed your baby if possible. It's so very easy for bottles and teats to be contaminated by germs – and this contamination is very nearly impossible from nice, clean nipples!

As I have mentioned, babies can become seriously dehydrated by diarrhoea or vomiting. So, in the case of a young baby, don't hesitate to seek medical advice.

Your GP will probably prescribe a mineral-rich powder, to which you add boiled water.

Antibiotics like penicillin will *not* help (as people so often imagine). Most D&V infections are caused by viruses – and viruses are the type of germs which are not affected by antibiotics. Indeed, some cases of diarrhoea can actually be made worse by antibiotics.

While the baby is on the boiled water mixture, don't succumb to the understandable temptation to give solids, or even milk. This is probably the commonest cause of a relapse of symptoms.

In really desperate cases of D&V, your GP will arrange admission to hospital. But in the average case, your baby's own defences against infection will enable him to defeat the bugs after a couple of days provided that he gets enough fluid (i.e. the boiled water mixture).

Toddlers, schoolchildren and adults will usually get better too within forty-eight hours or so, provided that they are given enough fluid. I repeat – don't attempt to give solids until the victim is completely better: all that'll happen is that the trouble will start again.

Kaolin mixture from the chemist's may be beneficial and some parents treat family outbreaks of diarrhoea with this themselves – but if a child's diarrhoea is really bad, you should always contact your GP.

Finally, remember that during the time that diarrhoea and vomiting is visiting your family, the affected members are all almost certainly putting out the germ in anything they vomit, and anything they pass from the back passage.

So it's more than ever important that you stick to the golden rules of loo and food hygiene outlined above. Take especial care with getting rid of soiled nappies. I'm afraid that again and again, doctors go into nice clean houses – and find a used nappy sitting on a table or the kitchen unit, just where it'll spread the D&V on!

Remember – at times like these, disposable nappies can be of immense value in stopping D&V from spreading round the family.

Alternative therapy

You *shouldn't* bother with alternative therapies in the case of a young baby with severe diarrhoea; she needs orthodox medical help – fast.

But in less severe and more long-standing cases, there is no harm in considering the idea of alternative treatment. **Homoeopaths** say that remedies such as phosphoric acid, podophyllum and 'China' are often curative. **Acupunc-**

turists claim that needling can speed recovery from acute diarrhoea, and help chronic cases. This is technically possible, in view of the current theory that acupuncture releases natural morphine-like pain-killers from the brain: it would be reasonable to expect these chemicals to have an anti-diarrhoea effect, just as morphine does (see *Acupuncture*).

Clinical ecologists hold that any child who has recurrent diarrhoea must be suspected of having a food allergy.

DISLOCATIONS

Children quite often dislocate joints – especially the joints of their fingers. Dislocation just means that the bone has temporarily popped out of its socket.

If this happens to your child, then the best thing to do is *not* to try and replace it yourself. Just immobilize the affected limb by gently bandaging it to a splint (i.e. something firm), and take the child to the nearest accident and emergency department so that the bone can be put back expertly and (I hope) with very little pain.

See also *Congenital dislocation of the hip.*

DIZZINESS

See *Giddiness.*

DOG BITES

These do seem to be getting more common, as more and more people buy large dogs for protection!

Fortunately, in Britain we still have no rabies. In many other countries, you should regard any dog bite as a possible source of this infection, and take the child to a doctor for anti-rabies shots.

Otherwise, treatment of a dog bite is as for cuts (see *First Aid*). The wound is quite likely to be dirty, so you should ask your doctor or the casualty department about anti-tetanus jabs.

However, the main thing is to reassure the child, who is liable to be badly frightened.

DOWN'S SYNDROME

Down's syndrome is an extraordinarily common form of mental handicap, occurring once in every 600 or 700 births.

It is also known as 'mongolism' – a term which is best not used nowadays, since it tends to distress parents of children with this condition.

The incidence is much greater in the babies of older mothers. In women over thirty-five years, the risk starts rising rapidly, reaching one in 50 if the expectant mother is aged forty-five. Many woman over the age of thirty-five ask for an amniocentesis test (which should detect Down's syndrome) if they become pregnant.

At present, the father's age is not thought to play a part. In a few cases, there is a family tendency to produce Down's children.

Babies with Down's syndrome have the facial appearance that everyone knows well. Unfortunately, this is accompanied by an IQ that nearly always lies between 25 and 50 (normal being 100). This makes any prospect of independent life quite impossible.

However, nearly all children with Down's syndrome are extraordinarily lovable and loving. It's often deeply touching to see how much their families adore them.

Admittedly, the stresses on some parents are truly colossal – and may lead to the break-up of the marriage. Other parents cope in the most incredible fashion, and some mothers and fathers go so far as to deny that their Down's children are severely handicapped at all. One can only admire such magnificent courage.

However, the fact is that the life expectancy of Down's syndrome youngsters is much less than normal. Quite a few have severe heart problems. Of those who survive to middle age, many develop premature senility. As their parents grow older or die, I'm afraid that institutional care often becomes necessary.

Alas, there is no *specific* treatment for Down's syndrome, and no drug that will 'improve' it. Shortly before this book went to press, claims were being made that Down's children could be helped by special waistcoats which are alleged to help pump more blood to the brain. These claims are almost certainly nonsense.

In fact, the only things which will help a Down's baby to develop are (a) love; and (b) constant stimulation by parents, family, friends, teachers and everybody else – to help the child learn as much as possible, and acquire as many skills as possible. Down's children should be integrated into playschools and other social groupings, just like all other children. They're very good mixers, and great fun to make

friends with. Parents should of course contact the self-help group:

The Down's Children's Association
4 Oxford Street
London W1

DREAMS, BAD

See *Nightmares*.

DROWNING

See *First Aid*.

DUST ALLERGY

Many children are allergic to dust – or (to be more accurate) to the tiny mites which so often live in housedust.

The symptoms which this allergy produces are really exactly the same as those of hayfever (see *Hayfever*), i.e. sneezing, runny nose and red, watery eyes.

Dust-mite allergy can't actually be cured but it can be controlled by the same sort of medications which are used for hayfever – nasal sprays such as Beconase and Rynacrom, and antihistamine pills. (*Caution*: these mostly make children sleepy.)

Naturally, you should also make every effort to reduce the amount of dust which the child comes into contact with. Removal of dust-attracting curtains, etc. may help, as should careful vacuuming of the bedroom and perhaps enclosing the mattress in plastic.

A preparation which is said to reduce the dust-mite population in carpets can be bought from chemists, and there is a vaccine against dust-mites but its value is still very uncertain.

DYSLEXIA

Dyslexia just means 'difficulty in reading'. It's important to grasp that this is a *symptom* – not a disease. There isn't really a medical disorder called dyslexia; it is a symptom of various disorders which all cause impairment, sometimes severe, of reading ability.

On the other hand, some of the children who have this symptom appear to have nothing else wrong with them. They're often bright and intelligent, but just lack this one skill.

So it must be assumed that their dyslexia is caused by a localized problem in the areas of the brain which deal with the written word. Despite intensive research, little more is known about the causes of this form of dyslexia, which has affected many otherwise clever and gifted people – among the most famous of whom is the actress Susan Hampshire.

Other dyslexic children do have clear-cut causes for their difficulty in reading – for instance, hearing or visual handicaps, epilepsy or emotional problems.

The important thing to realize is that if your child has dyslexia it does *not* mean that she is stupid!

If you suspect that your child is dyslexic, you must get your school to refer her to your local educational psychologist as soon as possible. Special help is available for dyslexic children in most areas these days – and by this I mean:

1   careful investigation and assessment by a multi-disciplinary team, including a clinical psychologist, a teacher with special experience in learning difficulties, and a doctor;
2   treatment – in the shape of intensive tuition in reading and writing, plus of course therapy for any underlying disorder.

With this kind of special help, many dyslexic children achieve remarkably good school results, and some of them have actually made very successful careers in jobs which involve the written word.

You should definitely contact the British Dyslexic Association at:

Church Lane
Peppard
Oxfordshire RG9 5JN

EAR ACHE

Ear ache ('otitis media') is an inflammation of the middle ear. This is the little cavity which lies behind the ear drum, and which contains the tiny bones that transmit the sounds we hear from the drum to the inner ear.

The inflammation is caused by germs – which don't get in through the 'ear hole' itself, but actually come up from the throat.

The middle ear cavity is connected to the throat by a narrow canal called the Eustachian tube. When a child has a sore throat or a cold, it's very easy for germs to find their way up this tube and into the ear. Once established there, they may cause inflammation and generate pus, thus producing pain. That's why so many kids have ear ache after a cold.

Sometimes too it can happen after a sudden descent in an aeroplane. This happened to two of my children on one holiday, which made the first three days pretty miserable for them. You can avoid this sort of trouble by getting your kids to 'clear their ears' by swallowing during airliner ascents and descents.

In some children there does seem to be a tendency to keep getting otitis media. When such a child gets a cold or tonsillitis, there's always a risk that, after two or three days, infection will become established in his ear. When this happens, he'll complain – loudly!

Of course, a two- or three-year-old can tell you where the pain is; but if your child is too young to talk, you may well have considerable difficulty in making out what's wrong with him. A baby with ear ache may hold his ear or keep rubbing it, but he may just scream, and keep screaming!

Very occasionally, a discharge of pus from baby's ear may indicate the likely cause of the trouble. What should put you on your guard as to the possibility of ear ache, however, is the baby's temperature. If it remains over 37·8°C (100°F) for several hours, and if he keeps screaming, then it's very likely that he has more than just an ordinary cold, and his ears should obviously be checked by a doctor. There's no need to dial 999 or to get the doctor to come instantly, but the child should be seen the same day. In the meantime, he must have adequate relief of his pain.

One simple pain-relieving measure is to place a hot water bottle wrapped in a cloth over the child's ear. With a baby or a very young toddler you mustn't do this in case you burn him. It may be better to use a hot pad, for instance, a towel heated on the radiator and re-placed by another every few minutes as it gets cold. An electric blanket applied to the ear region is ideal.

Second, give the child paracetamol or Panadol. If you use the junior type of paracetamol, give him the maximum dose for his age quoted on the packet (see *Paracetamol*).

Don't repeat the dose before four hours have elapsed, and please don't leave the tablets within the child's reach; remember that even junior paracetamol can be fatal.

Your GP may come and see the child or he may ask for him to be brought to the surgery. In the meantime, don't put either drops or cotton wool in the ear. The belief in the virtues of a solid plug of cotton wool dies hard in some parts of the world, but this really isn't a good idea, because it just provides a possible niche for germs to flourish in.

When the doctor sees your youngster, he'll inspect the child's ear drum with an instrument called an auriscope – and if he confirms that otitis media is present, he will put him on antibiotics.

It's very important to continue with these for the full course. Many doctors these days prefer to have a child on a ten- or fourteen-day course of penicillin or some other drug, but there is a tendency for some parents to think that they can stop the treatment after three or four days if the child seems better.

Slight deafness during an attack of otitis media is common. But some children's hearing is permanently affected afterwards, so it's a good idea to make a rough check a month or so after the attack. If your child has trouble hearing a whisper across a room, or a watch held close to his ear, ask your doctor to see him again and if necessary arrange a full hearing test (see *Deafness*).

A few ear, nose and throat specialists think that all children who've had ear ache should have a special hearing test (an audiogram) but this isn't practicable at the moment. Watch out for any sign of failing hearing, and take the child to your doctor if you are worried.

Alternative therapy

Because orthodox treatment, promptly given, is so effective, I'm very doubtful about recommending alternative therapy for this condition. However, **homoeopaths** believe in prescribing aconite, belladonna, camomile, sulphur and other non-toxic remedies.

ELECTRIC SHOCK

See *First Aid*.

ECZEMA

Hundreds of thousands of British children have eczema. Sadly, many of these kids go through a lot of unnecessary misery because people are unpleasant to them on account of the appearance of their skin – ('Come away, Johnny – don't play with that little boy in case you catch something!')

On the other hand, vast numbers of children only have very trivial eczema, which doesn't bother them, and which goes away as they get older. I don't mean to play down the distress suffered by people who have really bad eczema: I just want to make it clear that if your baby has a patch of eczema, you shouldn't worry about it, because there's a good chance that it'll disappear eventually.

Eczema is *not* an infection. Regrettably, many people see a patch of eczematous skin and think that it must be infectious. That's why a child with bad eczema may sometimes have a difficult time at school from unthinking classmates – and I've even heard of some ignorant teacher sticking a child with eczema in a corner 'so as not to infect the rest of the class'.

Doctors still don't entirely understand this disorder – or rather group of disorders, since there's more than one kind of eczema.

However, all of them are characterized by a kind of skin inflammation (or dermatitis) which is thought to be very often due to allergy.

This inflammation produces itchy red patches on the skin – often with uncomfortable cracks and a certain amount of oozing of fluid from the affected areas.

Babyhood eczema often starts at around the age of three months or so, and may come as a nasty shock to the mother – particularly if she's terribly proud of her new babe, and very upset by the idea of other people seeing a flaw in his appearance.

But if the patches of eczema aren't very extensive, there really is no cause for alarm. Small patches don't usually distress the child (as opposed to his Mum); he's blissfully unaware of them. So it's important to try and maintain a detached attitude if possible. I know it's easy for me to talk, but in fact two of my children had patches of eczema on their faces as young infants. Fortunately my missus – being a nurse and very philosophical – paid no attention to them and they eventually went away.

Having said all that, I must admit that big, raw itchy patches on the cheeks or forehead, or in the folds of the body (such as the inside elbow) can be distressing. Severe eczema of this sort definitely needs attention from your GP.

Your doctor will probably first of all advise you not to use soap and water on the affected areas. Understandably, many parents make the mistake of thinking that eczema is something to do with dirt, so they wash their poor infants enthusiastically. In fact, hot soapy water is the worst possible thing for eczematous skin. Liquid paraffin is a useful alternative for cleaning the affected area.

Bland creams of the Nivea type and tar ointments are often of some help, but if things are very bad your GP will prescribe one of the steroid (that is, cortisone-like) creams or ointments. You've probably heard of the well-known brands in this field, such as Betnovate and Synalar.

But be very sparing in using them – particularly on your child's face – because these steroids are extremely powerful. Used excessively, they can have serious side-effects – including permanent damage to the child's skin.

Also, try to find out what your baby is allergic to (remember, eczema is an allergic condition). Frankly, this isn't easy. But sometimes, by carefully trying the effect of excluding various foods in turn from the infant's diet, the mother discovers that one particular food seems to be making the child's skin worse.

Specialists in allergy now think that one of the most potent provokers of eczema is cow's milk. All bottle feeds are made from cow's milk, and no matter how wonderful the manufacturers may claim they are, they still contain proteins which are meant for little cows – not for little humans.

So recent research has shown that in families who have a tendency to allergy, there is a much greater chance of a baby getting infantile eczema if he's bottle-fed. Breast-feeding your baby has many advantages – and it's beginning to look more and more as if one of them is that you greatly reduce his chances of getting eczema.

If your baby develops eczema after several months of bottle-feeding, then obviously it's far too late to go back to the breast. But you could try giving him goat's milk or soya bean milk for a month or two – and if this doesn't work, get him on to fruit juices rather than cow's milk as soon as you can.

Finally, please bear in mind that the majority of cases of infantile eczema do get better, given time. One leading dermatologist estimates that only 5 per cent of affected babies will still suffer from eczema when they grow up. So when you look at those red weeping patches marring your otherwise beautiful baby's face, remember that they're most unlikely to be there for ever.

Eczema in a school-age child can be very trying, particularly as it so often affects the hands and the area round the mouth – both of which are very visible.

This prominence has helped to reinforce the idea that there is some psychological component in eczema. I suppose it's possible that just as blushing only affects the areas which people can see, eczema too is some kind of demonstration of inner emotions to the rest of the world. Certainly, it does seem to be true that when an eczematous child is upset, his skin gets worse.

On the other hand, parents shouldn't let themselves be carried away by the notion that eczema is all in the mind. It isn't. Just as in babyhood, eczema in the older child is usually an allergic disorder.

It's true that allergic youngsters are often a bit nervous and unsure of themselves. But the mere fact of having skin trouble which other children stare at is enough to make almost any child a bit anxious!

Just as in babyhood it is important to try and track down the allergen to which the child reacts. This isn't often successful, but if you do hit the jackpot and discover that your child's skin is made worse by eggs, milk, cheese, tea, coffee or whatever, then you've obviously made a great step forward.

In order to try to identify such an allergen, what you do is to stop the child from eating one particular foodstuff for a month or two, and see what happens. Keep a written record – including a record of how bad his skin is – so that you don't get confused when you come to look back at the results of your experiments. Take the record with you when you go to see your GP or dermatologist.

Things which come into contact with the skin can also be allergens, so it's worth trying to see if your child is allergic to metal (say, in a watch strap) or to rubber or to some particular material. Occasionally, a parent is lucky enough to find that the child's eczematous patches correspond exactly to the shape of some particular garment.

Changing your detergent is also well worth while, since it's quite common for children to be allergic to certain powders – particularly so-called biological ones.

Treatment prescribed by your doctor is likely to be on the same lines as that used for babies (see above). As with babies, be very careful not to overdo the steroid creams or ointments.

Finally, even if a child has bad eczema at the age of ten or twelve, there is still a reasonable chance that he may grow out of it. And if he doesn't, then bear in mind that the field of allergy is one area of medicine where very rapid progress is being made. In the other common allergic disorders (asthma and hayfever) great things have been achieved in developing specific anti-allergy drugs such as cromoglycate (Intal, Rynacrom or Lomusol). I think it's possible that similar advances will eventually be achieved in eczema. Until then, probably the most important thing is to reassure the poor child with eczema that he's not ugly or unpleasant or unloved! Parents will probably find it helpful to contact the National Eczema Society, whose address is:

57 Tavistock Place,
London WC1

Alternative therapy
Homoeopathic medicine advises gentle remedies such as sulphur. **Naturopathy** tends to rely on dietetic guidance (which is reasonable in view of the fact that many cases have an allergic basis). Similarly, **clinical ecologists** go for a food exclusion diet, concentrating on the exclusion of cow's milk, eggs, chicken and artificial preservatives from the child's diet.

ENURESIS

See *Bed-wetting*.

EPILEPSY

Epilepsy is common, and it causes a great deal of stress and grief for affected children (and their parents). Much of this is quite unnecessary and unfair – because it's caused by the prejudice of others. If we could get rid of this prejudice (and things *are* getting better – slowly!) life would be an awful lot easier for the child with epilepsy.

Now there are quite a lot of different types of epilepsy; it's not just one disease but lots of different ones. The two best-known types are petit mal and grand mal.

In petit mal the child just stops what he is doing and stares blankly into space for a little while, completely oblivious of what's going on around him. In such cases, you don't need to do anything in the way of first aid – just wait until he recovers.

Grand mal is more of a problem to cope with. This is the kind of fit in which the child falls down unconscious, shakes all over and may wet himself. It's very alarming for the watcher, particularly as the victim may look as though he's going to die. In reality, however, the child feels no pain or discomfort while the fit is going on – he's just as much out for the count as if he had been anaesthetized. Recovery will normally take place within a couple of minutes.

All you have to do is to place him on a soft comfortable surface where he can't injure himself, and turn him on his side. Loosen the clothing at his neck so that he can breathe easily as he comes round.

Don't try to jam anything between his teeth. This may prevent the child from biting his tongue – not usually a very serious occurrence, anyway – but it's also quite likely to lead to broken teeth (his) or bitten fingers (yours).

The only other first-aid measure you should remember is to take his temperature when he's recovered from the convulsion. If it's over about 38·6°C (101·5°F), strip his clothes off, sponge him down with tepid water, and give him some paracetamol to bring his temperature down (see *Feverish convulsions*).

Epilepsy is caused by an electrical storm in the brain; it's rather like an exaggeration of the sudden paroxysm of brain activity you or I experience when we sneeze. In some children, this disturbance happens because of brain damage at or before birth. In a very few, it's due to hereditary factors. But in most children with epilepsy we have no idea at all why this electrical storm should occur.

Among the cruel myths that surround the subject are age-old beliefs that epileptics are stupid, mentally deficient, insane or violent. They are none of these things.

Naturally, a child who is mentally handicapped because of brain damage sustained at birth may also have fits. However, the great majority of children with epilepsy are of average or even above-average intelligence. It's worth noting that Byron, Dante, Handel, Alexander the Great, Socrates, Julius Caesar and Dostoyevsky are all thought to have suffered from various forms of epilepsy.

However, as few people know these facts, the patient with epilepsy still has to face a great deal of prejudice and hostility. Recently, I've even come across several books which included thoughtless or light-hearted remarks that would have caused a great deal of pain to any sufferer from epilepsy who chanced to read them.

Certainly, if one of your children develops some form of epilepsy, you'll find that things are better than they used to be in schools. Most ordinary schools are very good these days about coping with a child who has convulsions, and only a small proportion of affected children have to go to a special school.

Once the diagnosis has been made, the child will be started on anticonvulsant drugs. There are many kinds available, and the paediatrician or neurologist (nerve specialist) will almost always have to experiment for some time before he finds the right combination and dose to suit a particular child's needs. It's absolutely essential that the pills or capsules are taken every day, exactly as prescribed. One of the commonest causes of recurrent fits is failure to take medication regularly; for example, when a patient decides that the pills aren't doing any good, or that they'd better be stopped because he has a cough or cold. This is very unwise.

Among children who are taking medication regularly, however, the results of treatment are very good. Between 80 and 90 per cent usually show a satisfactory degree of suppression of fits. Most parents find it's relatively easy to cope with a child who only has a few convulsions each year, though obviously it's necessary to take great care about such activities as cycling, swimming or horse-riding.

What about 'non-dangerous' sports? Here the child should be given a free rein. For years, epileptic children were cosseted and prevented from going in for physical activities like football or athletics, but that attitude has been completely changed by people like Tony Greig, the former England cricket captain, whose epilepsy didn't prove any handicap to him in his sport.

Job selection may be a problem, but very useful career advice as well as guidance on other aspects of epilepsy can be obtained from:

British Epilepsy Association
Crowthorne House
New Wokingham Road
Wokingham
Berkshire RG11 3AY

Another useful address is that of the National Society for Epilepsy, which does superb work in informing the public about epilepsy, and in running special schools for epileptic children. Its address is:

NSE
The Chalfont Centre
Gerrard's Cross
Bucks SL9 ORJ

See also *Hyperactivity*.

ERYSIPELAS

This is a skin inflammation, caused by a germ called the streptococcus, which is present in many children's throats and noses. The skin becomes reddened and hot, and feels hard to the touch. There is often fever, headache and vomiting. The infection usually responds well to antibiotic treatment.

Erysipelas used at one time to be quite a common condition, with a death rate of about 15 per cent. Nowadays it is very infrequently encountered, and deaths are very rare indeed.

FAINTING

Fainting isn't usually a sign of anything seriously wrong. Many healthy children – and adults – faint (look at guardsmen!).

A faint is caused by blood draining away from the brain – towards the legs and feet. This is particularly likely to happen if a child has just jumped up from a lying position, or if he's 'under the weather', or if it's very hot. Emotional stress can have the same effect.

Treatment is just simply to keep the child lying down till he's recovered. Resist the almost invariable tendency of 'helpful' bystanders to drag him into a sitting or upright position!

FAITH HEALING

No experienced doctor would deny that faith (in its various forms) can help to heal a person. Even where it doesn't heal, it can be of enormous assistance in strengthening morale and increasing the will to fight.

I have to say that miracle cures which can be ascribed to faith are rare. Take the example of Lourdes: literally thousands of children and adults go there every week – yet the Catholic Church only claims that about one apparently miraculous cure per year has occurred during the twentieth century. Nonetheless, the spiritual benefit to many sick children and their parents has clearly been enormous.

The type of spiritual healing to which so many parents turn in desperation is very difficult to evaluate. Simple laying on of hands by your local vicar or priest is often a great morale booster – but I

have known it to be desperately embarrassing to an older child!

I think you should beware of the razzmatazz, 'public hall' type of healing, which all too often has overtones of hysteria and commercial profit. Ask yourself carefully whether it's a good idea to take a child into such an atmosphere.

On the other hand, many people writing to me in my Agony Uncle capacity say that they or their children have received benefit from sincere healers, practising on a one-to-one basis, for no commercial motive. For more information, write to:

The Conference of Healing
   Organizations
c/o 113 Hampstead Way
London NW11

FATNESS

Yes, let's be blunt about it and use the word fatness, rather than the rather more polite 'being overweight'!

Far too many British children are almost hopelessly podgy. If you want to know whether your child is too fat, look at the illustration opposite. Your boy's or girl's weight should normally fall between the 'maximum' and 'minimum' lines indicated.

Only very rarely is this due to 'glandular trouble', as some fond parents claim. 999 times out of 1000, the trouble is that the child eats far too much high-calorie food (primarily fatty things). A secondary factor may be lack of exercise.

Some children eat too much because they're unhappy. Others are simply given far too large quantities by their

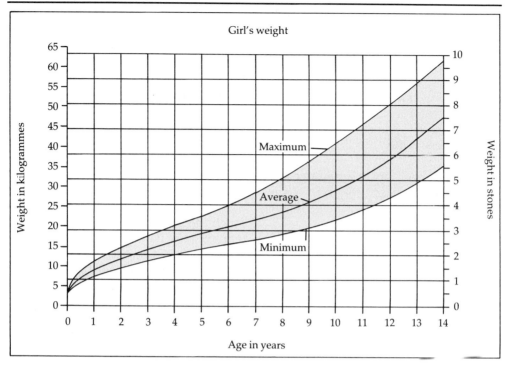

Girl's weight

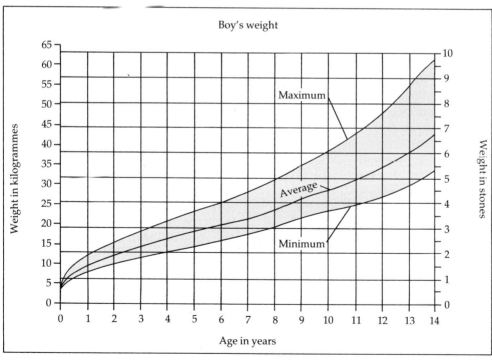

Boy's weight

parents – who often set the child a bad example by eating too much themselves.

So, if your child is too fat, set him a good example by cutting down on the stodgy, fatty things which you buy or cook. Take him to your doctor and get a strict diet sheet. If necessary, ask for an appointment with the local hospital dietitian.

But please don't try to pressurize your GP into putting your child on to 'slimming pills' – these are powerful, dangerous, and unlikely to work.

FEVER

See *Temperature*; also *Feverish convulsions*.

FEVERISH CONVULSIONS

NB For First Aid, see *First Aid* section.

If your youngster has a convulsion, or fit (as vast numbers of children do every year), your doctor will very likely tell you that she thinks it was just a feverish (or febrile) convulsion.

Most convulsions in childhood aren't caused by full-blown epilepsy (see *Epilepsy*), but by the effect of a raised temperature on the child's brain.

The young brain is very immature – and often quite unable to stand up to changes in temperature. (That's why children so readily become delirious when they're a bit hot.)

In many children, the brain simply cannot cope with a body temperature of more than about 38·9°C (102°F). So if the child has a bad cold or tonsillitis, and develops such a temperature, the brain responds by producing a convulsion.

Now it's important to distinguish these very very common feverish convulsions from convulsions which happen when a child *hasn't* got a raised temperature. The reason is that a convulsion which isn't caused by a high temperature may well have some more important cause – such as epilepsy. But in the case of a child whose convulsions are just feverish ones, the outlook is much better: most of them lose the tendency to having fits as they grow older. In fact, feverish convulsions are rarely seen above the age of five.

If your youngster has had just one feverish convulsion, your doctor may perhaps feel that it's unnecessary to subject him to a lot of investigation. But any child who's had more than one should definitely be investigated. Your GP will refer him to the local child specialist, who will examine him and carry out some tests – probably including an EEG (electroencephalogram) which is an electrical test of brain activity. It's quite painless.

In the light of the results he obtains, the specialist will advise you as to whether your child needs to take medicine or tablets every day in order to try to keep further fits away.

Now to the most important part of what I've got to say. For very understandable reasons, parents tend to make one serious error in looking after children with temperatures. When their youngsters are ill, they keep them too warm.

If your child has had a convulsion caused by a high temperature of, say, 38·9°C (102°F), then there is every chance that the next time he has a temperature of that level, he'll go into a convulsion again.

What happens in so many cases is that when a toddler has a bad cold or a cough, his parents wrap him up in lots of blankets, probably with a 'hotty', an electric fire in the room, and all the bedroom windows closed.

Of course, it is traditional to feel that you must keep a sick child as warm as possible, and doctors very often despair of persuading parents to keep feverish children *cool*.

Many's the time I've been to a house to treat a child with a temperature – only to have a frantic phone call a couple of hours later to say that 'the baby's having a convulsion!' In almost every case, the child has been so warmly wrapped that his temperature has shot up above the dangerous 38·9°C (102°F) level.

So if your child has already shown a tendency to feverish convulsions, then you will have to be prepared to bring his temperature down whenever he's feverish. Check his temperature every few hours. If it's above 38·3°C (101°F) taken by mouth, then he must be cooled down until his temperature is well below danger levels. Give him a little paracetamol, and remove any woolly underwear, thick blankets or eiderdowns. If you just let him lie under a sheet, in a reasonably cool bedroom, this will probably be enough to bring his temperature down.

If his thermometer reading is still the same after half an hour or so, however, then you should carry out the procedure known as tepid sponging. This just means spending a few minutes wiping his limbs and body down with coolish water – a process which, I'm afraid, he may not like all that much. It may also be helpful to play an electric fan on him if you have one.

These measures will cool most children who have a tendency to convulsions, and take them out of the danger area on the thermometer. Do not be swayed by relatives' opinions: by cooling your child down, you are actually doing the best possible thing for your child – and not giving him pneumonia!

Note: teething does *not* cause convulsions, whatever anyone may say.

FIBROCYSTIC DISEASE

See *Cystic fibrosis*.

FIFTH DISEASE (*Erythema infectiosum*)

This is a very common childhood infection, though its name is almost unknown to the public for some reason. This is odd, because very large numbers of children get this condition.

The word disease doesn't imply that the illness is serious – it isn't. And it's called 'fifth disease' because it was discovered after four other common causes of fever and rash in childhood (German measles, measles, roseola and chickenpox) had been identified.

It's recently been shown that fifth disease is almost certainly due to a virus. The incubation period is seven to fourteen days, after which the child may develop a slight temperature and perhaps a sore throat.

But what is really striking is the rash. This looks exactly as if the child has been hit across the face – which is why this is sometimes known as Slapped Cheek Syndrome.

Parents may be quite alarmed by this appearance, but the doctor should be able to reassure them that all is well. A net-like rash will usually spread to the backs of the hands and arms, and to the buttocks and legs. Aches in the joints sometimes occur.

No treatment is necessary (other than perhaps calamine lotion if the rash is itchy). The child will invariably get better within a few days.

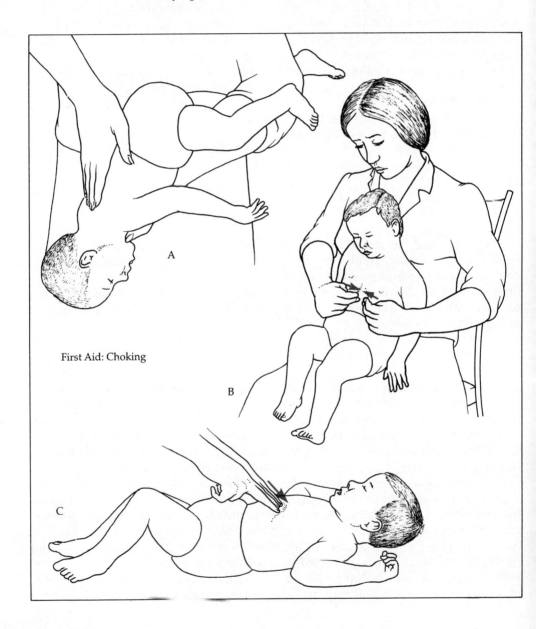

First Aid: Choking

FIRST AID

Note: the advice given here is meant FOR FAST READING IN CASES OF EMERGENCY. Obviously, there's a lot more to first aid care than I can include here – and I'd strongly recommend all parents to learn more (and so prepare themselves for trouble!) by taking one of the excellent courses run by the British Red Cross, St John Ambulance Brigade or (in Scotland) St Andrew's Ambulance.

BLEEDING

In cases of heavy bleeding, the one really vital thing is immediately to press something (preferably a clean cloth) really firmly on to the bleeding point. Keep pressing – and do not let up till expert help arrives.

Don't put on tourniquets, as these are liable to cause gangrene, and so may cost the child a limb. (For less heavy bleeding, see *Cuts and grazes*, below.)

BURNS AND SCALDS

The moment you realize a child has been burned (or scalded), drench the affected part in cold water immediately. If there are smouldering clothes on the skin, cut them off before they do more damage.

Remove any bangles or rings, as the skin may start swelling up.

In the case of a large burn, *don't* apply anything: cover the part with a very clean cloth, and get the child to medical help.

In the case of a small burn, you can safely apply any of the standard antiseptic creams or ointments.

CHOKING

When a child chokes, she tries to inhale air but can't – because there's something in the way. Nearly always, this is a foreign body lodged in the upper part of the windpipe. If no air gets in at all, the child will go very dark, and die within a few minutes.

In the case of a baby or toddler, hold her upside down and get someone to slap her back gently (see picture (A) opposite). In the case of an older toddler or schoolchild, use Heimlich's manoeuvre: either hold him on your lap (B), or lie him on a firm surface (C), and thrust your finger tips into his upper tummy.

It's occasionally possible for an adult with a long finger to hook a foreign body out of a child's throat – but it's difficult.

CONVULSIONS

Lie the child on his side. Loosen the clothing round his neck. Stay with him and protect him from injury till he recovers or help arrives.

Don't try to push things between his teeth. See also *Feverish convulsions*, and *Epilepsy*.

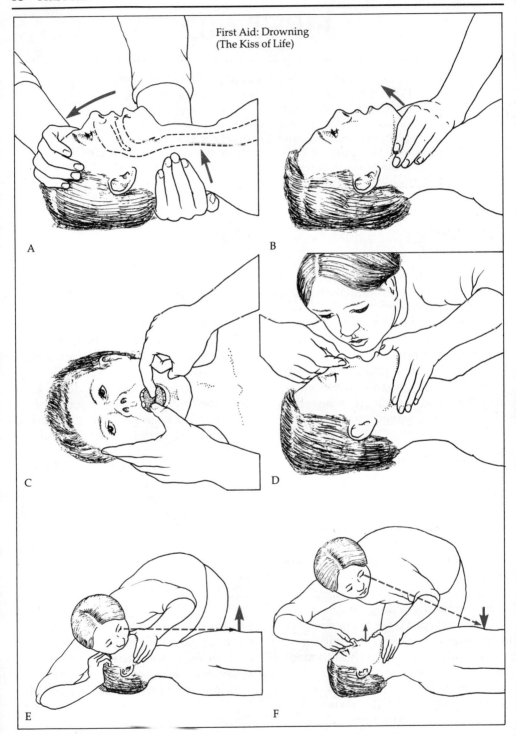

First Aid: Drowning
(The Kiss of Life)

A

B

C

D

E

F

CUTS AND GRAZES

Control bleeding as described under *Bleeding* (above). Once that's under control, wash the injured part – preferably in warm water. Try to get any bits of grit out. Dab dry with a clean towel.

In the case of a large graze, it's probably worth applying one of the standard antiseptic creams or liquids. Sealed sterile plasters are ideal for covering childhood cuts.

If a cut is deep or dirty, ask a doctor whether a tetanus jab is needed.

DROWNING

Speed may save the child's life. Get him out of the water – ideally on a slope with his head down (positioned as shown in picture (A) opposite), making sure his head is tilted well back (B). Clear his mouth of any seaweed, sand or vomit (C). Close off his nose with your finger and thumb (D), place your mouth over his mouth (in the case of a baby, his mouth and nose) and give the kiss of life: blow in gently (E) – you'll see his chest rise; let the air come out again (F) – you'll see his chest fall.

If his heart seems to have stopped (feel for a pulse at the front of the neck), you must give heart massage – as shown in the picture overleaf.

ELECTRIC SHOCK

A minor shock is very frightening but will do no harm. Unless the child is burned, there's no need to do more than console her.

A serious shock may kill the child – and the rescuer. First turn the current off. If the child is unconscious, check that she's breathing. If not give the kiss of life – see opposite. Check if her heart is beating – if not, give heart massage – see overleaf.

If breathing and heartbeat are OK, keep the child in the 'coma position' (see *Unconsciousness* p. 72) and call an ambulance.

GAS POISONING *(Gassing)*

Since we went over to natural gas this is now rare in Britain. But it does occur in caravans, boats and other enclosed living quarters with badly ventilated heaters. Victims are found unconscious, and often bright pink.

Immediate action: drag the child into clean air quickly (before you yourself are overcome!). Give the kiss of life (see opposite). If his heart has stopped, give heart massage (see overleaf).

HEAD INJURIES

Head injuries can kill. Even a heavy blow from a fist can be fatal to a youngster.

So, if a child is knocked out, put him in the 'coma position' (see *Unconsciousness* p. 72).

When he comes round, he *must* be seen by a doctor. It's a definite rule (which few parents are aware of), that if a youngster has been KOd (even for a brief period) he should be taken to hos-

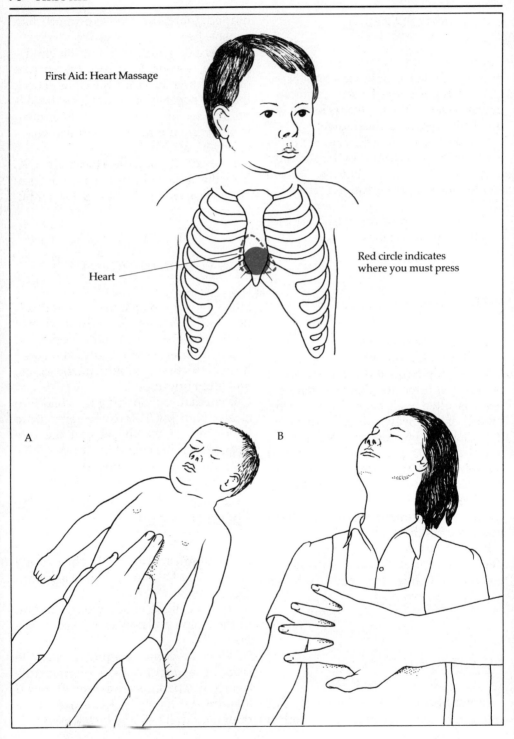

First Aid: Heart Massage

Heart

Red circle indicates
where you must press

A

B

pital, x-rayed, *and admitted for a night's observation.*

Kiss of Life
See the picture sequence and *Drowning* pp. 68–9.

Heart Massage *(Cardiac Massage)*
See the illustrations opposite. With a baby (A): place her on a firm surface, put the tips of two fingers on her breastbone, press *down* sharply and release – at a rate of about 100 times a minute. With an older child (B): place the flat of one hand on her breastbone, press *down* sharply and release – at a rate of about 80 to 100 times a minute.

POISONING

For poisoning by gas, see *Gas Poisoning* (p. 69).

Treat any case of poisoning as potentially fatal. Never wait to see how things go just because the child seems quite well, or because you think he hasn't taken very much. Always take the poison or the empty container to hospital with you; if the child has vomited, take a specimen of the vomited material as well.

The unconscious patient Turn him on his side, and remove anything (vomit, etc.) blocking the mouth. Make sure he can breathe, as described below in *Unconsciousness.*

Then phone for an ambulance. Delay in getting the child to hospital may be fatal.

The conscious patient If the child has swallowed a corrosive poison (i.e. an acid or alkali), or a petroleum product, do *not* make him vomit. (If he is scream-ing in pain, this probably indicates that he has swallowed a corrosive.) Dilute the poison by giving him water to drink. If his mouth or face have been burned by the corrosive, splash water liberally across the skin to wash all traces of it away. Then lie him down and phone for an ambulance.

Most poisons (including all medicinal pills and tablets) are not corrosive. Here the first thing to do is to encourage the conscious child to vomit, either by poking fingers down his throat or, if this fails, by giving a drink of salt water (or mustard in water). Then get him to hospital as fast as possible. (If he is still conscious and free from pain, there is no reason why you should not use an ordinary car rather than an ambulance to save time.)

Note: don't waste time searching for antidotes. These seldom exist outside the pages of fiction (and somewhat elderly fiction at that).

STINGS

Bee stings These are rarely serious. If the sting is still in the skin, remove it gently with a pair of tweezers or the blade of a knife. Don't squeeze the skin. In fact, if you leave things completely alone after removing the sting, the inflammation should soon be gone. Occasionally, the pain may be quite severe – if so, apply a pad of cotton wool dipped in cold water to the skin and give some paracetamol.

In cases of multiple bee stings (which may happen if a whole swarm of bees attacks somebody) or stings in the mouth, consult a doctor as soon as possible.

A small number of children are allergic to bee stings, and in such patients collapse and even sudden death may occur after a single sting. If a child who has been stung collapses, rush him to hospital, and be prepared to give the kiss of life (see p. 68 and under *Drowning*) if breathing stops.

Wasp stings These too, are usually fairly trivial. Consult a doctor, however, if the sting is in the mouth. There is no actual sting to remove from the skin.

Cold compresses and paracetamol can be used to relieve pain. It's traditional to put mild acids (vinegar or lemon juice) on wasp stings, and mild alkalis (such as bicarbonate of soda) on bee stings, but there's no evidence that this is helpful. Pain-relief sprays, such as Wasp-eze, are useful.

If collapse occurs treat as described under *Bee stings*, above.

UNCONSCIOUSNESS

It's alarming to find a child unconscious. But keep your head – because calm, sensible action by you may save her life.

An unconscious child could choke to death – particularly if her tongue falls back and blocks her airway. So put the child into the first-aider's 'coma position' (see picture below). This helps to prevent her tongue from falling back and blocking her throat. You should also clear her mouth of anything which may be blocking it (such as blood clots, road debris or vomit).

If there's no sign of breathing, you must then turn the child on her back and give the kiss of life (see under *Drowning* on p. 69).

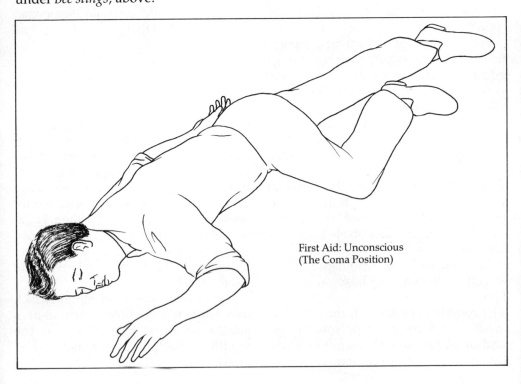

First Aid: Unconscious
(The Coma Position)

FITS

See *Epilepsy*; also *Feverish convulsions*.

FLAT FEET

This common condition is one in which the arches (curves) under the child's feet simply aren't high enough. This means that her wet footprint looks like drawing B instead of drawing A below.

The cause of flat feet isn't known. Fortunately, the condition doesn't matter all that much – though you have to accept that it means your child isn't likely to be a champion Olympic sprinter. An orthopaedic surgeon will tell you whether any treatment is really desirable or not. Possible treatments include foot exercises, supports in the shoes and surgery.

FLEA BITES

People are liable to get very sensitive about being told that their child has flea bites! However, these bites are still pretty common in Britain today – though nearly always now, it's the cat flea (rather than the human variety) which causes them.

These bites produce very itchy and annoying little reddish bumps, which tend to be on the child's palms (presumably from stroking the cat) and on his calves (where the cat rubs against them).

Get treatment for your cat – not your child! The vet will advise you about flea

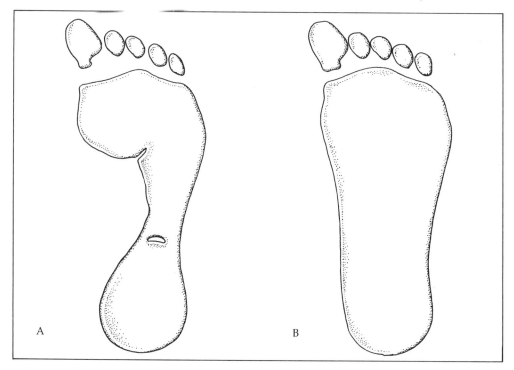

A   B

sprays and flea collars, and will empha-
size the importance of spraying places
(cushions, baskets, etc.) where the cat
likes to lie.

FOOD POISONING

This is caused by germs, and is getting
disturbingly common in Britain. This is
partly because, astonishingly, most of
the frozen birds (and some of the frozen
sausages) you buy in shops are contaminated with salmonella germs!
These are only killed if you follow these
strict rules:
1 don't put frozen poultry or meat
   where it can drip on other foods;
2 don't put it on working surfaces
   which you're then going to use for
   other foods;
3 defrost it very thoroughly;
4 cook it thoroughly too.
Other good rules for preventing food
poisoning are:
5 don't let anyone with an infected
   finger or hand prepare food;
6 make sure all food-handlers in your
   home wash their hands after going
   to the loo;
7 don't leave warm meat dishes around
   (particularly uncovered ones) to cool
   slowly, with a view to re-heating
   them later. Put them in the fridge –
   or else cook only small portions, because these will cool faster.
Symptoms of food poisoning include
tummy ache, diarrhoea and vomiting
(see *Diarrhoea* and *Vomiting*). If you suspect food poisoning in your family, put
the victims to bed, call a doctor – and if
possible save the food so that tests can be
done if necessary.
See also *Fungus poisoning*.

FRACTURES

Fracture means exactly the same as
break. Broken bones are common in
childhood, more so in boys than in girls.
Fortunately, most fractures are simply
very painful, rather than terribly serious.
If you suspect a broken bone:
• immobilize the affected bit of your
  child, as in the pictures opposite – by
  gently splinting it to something firm
  (e.g. a walking stick).
• take him to the nearest accident and
  emergency department, since an
  x-ray will nearly always be needed.
• don't give him any food or drink.
If the x-ray shows that the fracture
hasn't caused any deformity of the
bone, the doctor will probably put on a
plaster of Paris (or similar immobilizing
arrangement) to keep the bone ends
steady till they knit together.
If the fracture has caused a deformity
of the bone, then the doctor will have to
'reduce' it. This just means putting the
bone straight, and it has to be done
under a general anaesthetic. This is why
you should not give any food or drink to
a child who has a possible fracture!
The doctor will put on the plaster cast
(or similar support) while the child is
unconscious.
Most fractures take very roughly six
weeks to knit together, but this varies
depending on the site and the degree of
damage.

FUNGUS POISONING

Never give your children 'mushrooms'
picked in a field – just in case they're
poisonous fungi.

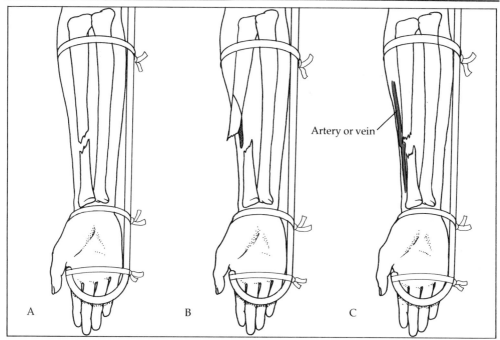

A. Ordinary fracture B. 'Compound' fracture – i.e. one in which the skin is broken
C. 'Complicated' fracture – i.e. one in which the bone has damaged another structure

Symptoms of fungus poisoning include diarrhoea, vomiting, abdominal pain and collapse.

If you ever suspect that this has happened to your child, get her to hospital fast (preferably taking a specimen of the fungi with you).

GAS POISONING

See *First Aid*.

GASTRITIS

This is an irritation of the stomach, uncommon in children except when it is caused by the sort of germs which cause them to vomit (see *Diarrhoea* and *Vomiting*).

GASTROENTERITIS

This is an irritation of the stomach *and* intestines by germs – with resulting diarrhoea and vomiting. See *Diarrhoea; Vomiting;* also *Food poisoning*.

GERMAN MEASLES (*Rubella*)

This is a mild infection for a child, but possibly a very serious one for an expectant Mum.

Children catch the rubella virus from other people who have it – the virus is sprayed out as an infected child or adult breathes, sneezes, laughs or talks. It then enters somebody else's nose or mouth – and that's it.

About fourteen to twenty days later,

the youngster probably gets German measles.

Symptoms vary wildly; an affected child may not have any obvious symptoms at all. She may not even have a rash. (This is why so many adults turn out to be immune to rubella when their blood tests are done – even though they don't remember having had it as children!)

But many children with German measles do have a rash – a bumpy brownish-pink one (see picture opposite). It doesn't develop heads, and it's not particularly itchy.

At the same time, the child may be slightly off-colour, possibly with a mild sore throat. A good clue is that the glands at the back of his neck are usually enlarged.

Your doctor should see the child to confirm the diagnosis – but please *don't* take him down to the surgery, where he might encounter expectant mothers.

No treatment is needed, but your doctor will presumably advise keeping him at home for at least a few days, for fear of infecting pregnant women (see below).

In Britain, all girls are offered the German measles vaccine before puberty – and your daughter should take advantage of this jab, even though she may have been diagnosed as having German measles earlier in life. In the USA, all children (girls and boys) are given the vaccine, which seems very sensible.

Adults quite often catch rubella from children (though in fact 80 per cent of adults are immune.) The infection can be more severe in grown-ups, and may cause quite unpleasant joint pain in the hands and feet.

More importantly, it can cause appalling abnormalities in unborn babies – which is why an expectant mother

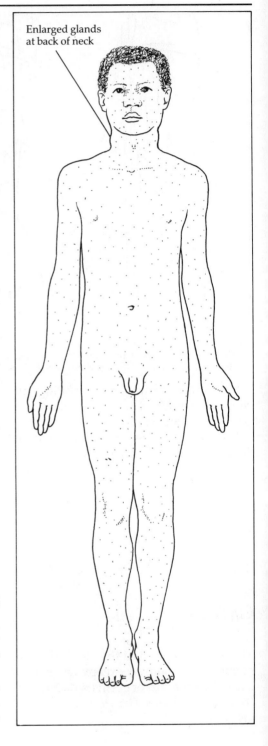

Enlarged glands at back of neck

(especially in early pregnancy) should not go near a child with rubella.

Ideally, all women of child-bearing age should have been immunized against rubella. (NB. This must *not* be done in pregnancy.) If you are pregnant and you come into contact with a child with German measles, ask your doctor to do a blood test to check whether you're at risk.

GIDDINESS

This isn't often a serious symptom in children. It may occur when a child is under emotional pressure, or when she's generally under the weather and about to go down with some virus illness.

However, if your child keeps on complaining of dizzy spells over a long period of time, she should be checked over by your GP.

GLANDULAR (*Infectious*
FEVER   *Mononucleosis*)

This virus infection is common in teenagers and young adults – and occasionally occurs in schoolchildren.

The virus is believed to be spread from mouth to mouth by talking, laughing, sneezing, coughing – and perhaps kissing!

Infectious mononucleosis (mono, as it's known in the USA) is thought to come on about 1½ weeks after exposure. The symptoms are tiredness and weakness, fever, sore throat and swollen glands. The diagnosis can be confirmed with a blood test.

Recovery may unfortunately take some months, during which the child will just have to take life moderately easy. He should be excused school games.

There is no special treatment, because viruses don't respond to antibiotics. In particular, *don't* let anyone give your child ampicillin (Penbritin) – because this antibiotic very often produces a really unpleasant, itchy rash when given to a child with glandular fever.

Finally, bear in mind that you may have to take special trouble to be kind and easy-going with your youngster after a bout of glandular fever. It may be some months before he feels totally well again, and the tiredness may affect both his behaviour and his school work.

GRAZES

See *Abrasions* and *First Aid* (*cuts and grazes*).

GROWING PAINS

These don't exist. If your child gets aches and pains in her joints or bones, have her checked out by your GP.

GROWTH

The approximate rates at which your child should grow are shown in the two tables overleaf. In general, a child's height and weight should be within the 'maximum' and 'minimum' bands shown here and under *Fatness*.

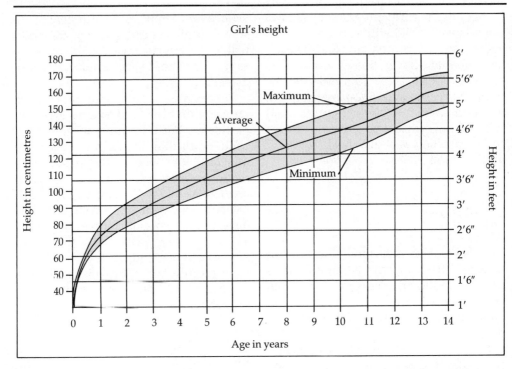

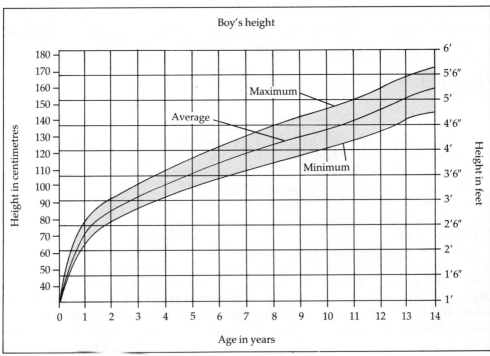

You may like to plot your youngster's development on the graphs. As a rule, her growth curves should maintain roughly the same position within the bands. If there's an unexplained flattening out (in other words, failure to gain), you should check with your doctor or – in the case of small children – your child health clinic.

GUM DISORDERS

Gum disorders aren't common in children, provided they clean their teeth at least once daily and see their dentist twice a year.

But bleeding gums may indicate a problem, and should be checked out by a dental surgeon.

Large, painful lumps on the gum are usually abscesses caused by infection from decayed teeth: the child should see a dentist fast, so that the abscess can be dealt with.

HAIR LOSS

See *Alopecia*.

HALITOSIS

See *Bad breath*.

HARE LIP

See *Cleft palate*.

HAYFEVER

This is very common in childhood, especially in 'allergic' families. (So, too, is the closely related condition called dust-mite allergy, see *Dust Allergy*).

Typically, the child develops running eyes, and starts sneezing and snuffling in the grass pollen season – which in Britain may arrive in April or May, depending on the weather. (In other countries, hayfever may arrive at other times – in the USA, it happens during the ragweed pollen season.)

The diagnosis is usually obvious, though some kids are wrongly thought to have 'recurrent colds'.

Treatment has improved a lot recently. These are the main types of therapy:

- older anti-histamine pills and medicine. These have the disadvantage of making many children sleepy (a big problem if there are school exams in May or June!);
- newer anti-histamines – which have no real sedative effect;
- steroid inhalers, such as Beconase (very useful, and no sedation);
- nasal anti-allergy drugs, such as Rynacrom or Lomusol (cromoglycate). A version of this can be used in the child's eyes, to combat the disabling wateriness and redness. (Note that these drugs *must* be used long-term for their protective effect – it's no good trying to use them to treat a sudden attack of hayfever.)
- desensitizing jabs. These can occasionally cause serious, or even fatal, collapse. Their results are variable, so you have to think carefully before you decide whether you want your child to have a series of 'needles'.

But don't forget these commonsense ways of combatting hayfever:

- if possible keep your windows closed on warm, dry days – when the pollen count is likely to be high;
- ditto with car windows;
- consider wrap-around sunglasses to keep the pollen out of your child's eyes;
- if things are really awful, experiment with a cowboy game in which he wears an outlaw's bandanna over his nose and mouth;
- if you're desperate, remember that there's likely to be less pollen: in air-conditioned rooms; at the swimming baths; and in a boat out at sea!

Alternative therapy
Homoeopathic medicine uses such agents as teucrium, sabadilla and mixed pollens to treat hayfever. **Clinical ecologists** quite rightly believe in shielding the child from pollen, and may also attempt to relieve rhinitis (nose inflammation) by food exclusion and/or desensitization.

HEAD INJURY

See *First Aid*.

HEADACHE

Headache is common in children but isn't usually serious, except in rare cases (see, for instance, *Meningitis*).
Possible causes include:

- any feverish illnesses (colds, 'flu, etc.)
- sinusitis (see *Sinusitis*)
- tension (yes, children get it too)
- head injury (see *First Aid*)

- migraine (see *Migraine*).

Eye strain is often said by adults to be a cause of headache, but this seems a bit doubtful. However, if your child has recurrent headaches, it certainly does no harm to have his eyes checked by an optician.

For donkeys' years, constipation was supposed to be a cause of headache, but that now seems highly doubtful, partly because constipation is at the wrong end of the body to produce a headache.

Parents quite naturally worry about brain tumours in children who have recurrent headaches, but these are actually quite rare.

Don't encourage your child to think he has a headache – if you worriedly say 'Have you got a headache, darling?' to a child who's a bit below par, there's a fair chance that he'll decide that he has! After a while, having a headache may become a major part of his life.

But if he does seem to have a headache, check his temperature (see *Temperature*) in case he's brewing up a feverish illness.

If his temperature is normal and there are no other symptoms, then just encourage him to go out in the fresh air, rather than lie around!

But if the headache persists for more than an hour, give him paracetamol (in the dose recommended for his age on the packet).

If the headache persists for more than five or six hours, or if it's accompanied by an unexplained temperature, then ring your doctor.

HEART TROUBLE

This is fortunately now very rare in children in Britain. Whereas rheumatic heart disease used to be common up until the 1950s (see *Rheumatic fever*), it is now very unusual.

Congenital abnormalities of the heart do occur in babies, usually for no known reason. More common abnormalities are: holes in the heart; misshapen positioning of the tubes leading into or out of the heart. Fortunately, many of these abnormalities can now be corrected by surgery – even possibly by heart transplantation in a few cases.

Cardiomyopathy is the term used to indicate one of a group of disorders in which there's a serious abnormality of the muscle which makes up the heart. In childhood cases, the cause is virtually always unknown. Treatment is with drugs to help the ailing heart muscle to pump. In a few cases a heart transplant is a possibility.

HEARTBURN

See *Indigestion*.

HERBALISM

This is a very popular form of alternative therapy. There are many herbalists in Britain – and many shops which sell 'herbal remedies' for minor childhood illnesses.

The great thing about herbal remedies is that most of them do seem to be pretty mild – so that the chance of side-effects is pretty low, *provided* that you only give your child the recommended doses.

But it's a mistake to fall into the trap of thinking that because herbal remedies are natural, they must be totally harmless. If a herb can have an effect on your child's body, then it's inevitable that too much of it could be bad for her. For instance, the classic case of a herbal remedy which turned out to be wonderfully useful was the foxglove (digitalis). Extract of foxglove proved to be a lifesaver for many people with weak hearts. But too much of it would kill your child (or you) very quickly indeed.

In practice, overdose of herbal remedies seems to be very rare in Britain – though in the tropics I have encountered serious side-effects from over-use of herbal remedies.

If you decide to take your child to a herbal practitioner, do make sure that it's somebody who's properly qualified. Members of the National Institute of Medical Herbalists carry the letters MNIMH or FNIMH after their names. For a full list of such practitioners, send a large sae to:

> Hon. General Secretary
> NIMH
> 41 Hatherley Road
> Winchester
> Hampshire

HERNIA

This is the same thing as rupture. In other words, it's a condition where part of a child's insides start bulging through a weak spot somewhere.

The common weak spots are (a) the groin; (b) the navel.

Groin hernias These are quite common in young children – especially boys. The symptom is a bulge, just about where the inner thigh meets the trunk. This may or may not be painful.

These childhood hernias can't really be palliated with trusses or other methods. In general, by far the best thing is to arrange to have the hernia operated on.

This isn't a big operation: the surgeon will close the gap and (with luck) the child will only have a very tiny scar.

Navel (umbilical) hernias   The navel tends to be a weak place, and young babies frequently have a mild hernia there. For some reason, these little ruptures are specially common in babies of African/West Indian extraction.

Fortunately, very small bulges will often go away as the child's tummy muscles get stronger. (An old remedy was to strap a coin over the bulge to try and make it go away, but I doubt if this does anything!)

If the hernia doesn't disappear, it must be operated on. One older operation involves removing the navel altogether, which is distressing for a child, since other youngsters are bound to say 'Oi! You ain't got no belly button!'

So talk the procedure over with the surgeon *first*, and be certain what is going to be done before you sign the consent form.

HICCUPS

All children get hiccups, usually due to their stomachs being a bit overstretched by food.

Most cases of hiccups stop by themselves. Where this doesn't happen, it's worth trying traditional remedies like drinking out of the wrong side of a glass or putting a tiny spot of salt on the child's tongue (but only if *she* agrees!).

Very rarely, hiccups go on for many hours, and this can be very tiring and distressing. In these cases, the child should be seen by a doctor – who may try prescribing a sedative or muscle relaxant.

Alternative therapy
Homoeopaths use remedies like nux vomica and ginseng to treat hiccups.

HIP, CONGENITAL
DISLOCATION OF

See *Congenital dislocation of hip*.

HIVES

See *Urticaria*.

HODGKIN'S DISEASE

This serious disorder of the lymph glands affects some young adults and older children. The cause isn't known.

Symptoms include painless swelling of the glands in the neck, armpits and groin; weakness; and sometimes jaundice.

Hodgkin's disease isn't the same as leukaemia, though the two diseases are linked in many people's minds. In fact, the outlook is decidedly better in Hodgkin's disease, and most children who get it can now be cured – though the cure will take some years. Treatment is with powerful anti-cancer-type drugs and radiotherapy.

Holiday immunizations

See *Immunization*.

Homoeopathy

Homoeopathy is probably the most favourably regarded form of alternative medicine among doctors – mainly because we're well aware that it can't do anybody any harm! (I don't think that most doctors have the least objection to the fact that members of the Royal Family have had a homoeopathic physician, among the other royal doctors, for many years.)

The reason why homoeopathy is so safe is that the medicine which homoeopathic doctors use are so very diluted – so diluted, in fact, that orthodox doctors often doubt whether there's anything of the original medicine left among all that water!

Homoeopathy is based on the teachings of Samuel Hahnemann, a nineteenth-century doctor who believed that 'like cured like'. In other words, he thought that if your child had a fever, it was a good idea to treat her with a natural remedy which *also* tends to cause fever.

You might have thought that this would cause problems – by making the symptoms worse. But Hahnemann's idea was that the natural remedy should be greatly diluted – a million million times or more! This certainly does avoid any question of side-effects.

Homoeopathic doctors work on the same principles today. One reason why patients (and parents) often favour them is that they usually take immense trouble over obtaining a careful history, sometimes spending an hour or two in building up a picture of the whole patient.

Another good point about homoeopathic doctors is that they accept the need for orthodox treatment in many cases. In other words, if your child has appendicitis, a homoeopathic doctor will probably call in a surgeon to remove the appendix.

I've mentioned various homoeopathic remedies in this book. But although many people do treat themselves and their children homoeopathically, I don't think you should attempt this unless you really know what you're doing.

It's better to take your child to a doctor who is also homoeopathically qualified. Names of such doctors can be obtained from:

The British Homoeopathic
  Association
27A Devonshire Street
London W1N 1RJ

(Please enclose sae.)

Hydrocephalus

This means 'water on the brain' – a serious condition mostly occurring in the first year of life. The classic symptom is marked enlargement of the child's skull. This is caused by a blockage of the drainage tube through which brain fluid (CSF) normally drains away.

Unfortunately, the rising pressure within the skull very often affects the child's brain, and may therefore affect her intelligence.

Hydrocephalus is not easy to treat,

but the position was improved many years ago when an American engineer whose own child was dying of hydrocephalus sat down and designed a brilliantly simple valve which could be implanted into the child's body by a surgeon – and which would drain off the excess fluid.

With the aid of this device and its successors (and also with drug treatment) the lives of many babies with hydrocephalus have been saved.

For further information, write (enclosing an sae) to:

> Association for Spina Bifida and
>   Hydrocephalus
> Tavistock House North
> Tavistock Square
> London WC1

HYPERACTIVITY

Hyperactivity just means having too much activity or energy. Now *all* children are far too active at times – and wear their parents into a frazzle as a result!

But beware of assuming that your child is hyperactive, just because he wears you out. In the USA (though not yet in Britain) there's a most unfortunate tendency for parents, teachers and even some doctors to regard any child who isn't thoroughly placid all the time as hyperactive. Crazy as this may seem, thousands of these children have been put on powerful drugs to try to calm them down – and inevitably some of them have suffered as a result of unwanted side-effects.

It is even said that some allegedly hyperactive children have undergone brain surgery in the USA in order to make them more 'disciplined'.

I'm afraid that some doctors, even in the UK, have a slight tendency to put a boisterous or noisy child on a powerful tranquillizer or sedative to calm him down a bit. Personally, I think that parents ought to be extremely cautious about this – especially as a child often gets even more uncontrollable if adults are daft enough to fill him up with Valium (or whatever). Of course, there are a very few children whose excessive activity goes far beyond the bounds of the normal. They are on the go from morning till night, frequently playing in a destructive, aggressive and noisy way, making a point of breaking things or of hurting other people. They may be extremely difficult for a teacher or a parent to handle.

There is usually some good reason for such extraordinary behaviour. The main reasons are as follows:

- brain damage;
- autism (see *Autism*);
- severe epilepsy (see also *Epilepsy*);
- psychological problems.

In brain-damaged children the damage has usually taken place either at birth or in the womb. Often these children are severely deficient mentally and have to spend their lives in an institution; however, a lot of children with less severe brain damage are perfectly capable of a happy and independent life. But some of them do have a type of brain damage that tends to make them overactive, noisy and rather irresponsible. This is very trying for their parents and teachers, but is something that has to be faced. Though drugs may sometimes help, the most important thing is to show the child plenty of love and understanding.

Bear in mind that there is often a large psychological element to the over-activity. Like the children with emotional problems (see below), the child with brain damage may be showing his aggression in a desperate attempt to find love.

Children with severe epilepsy are far more common – and many of these children are (for some time at least during their childhood) decidedly hyperactive. There are several possible reasons for this. First, children with severe epilepsy do sometimes have some sort of brain damage.

Second, nearly all youngsters with epilepsy are on some kind of drugs (to prevent fits) and these drugs can make a child both irritable and hyperactive. Happily, some of the newer drugs are much less likely to cause behaviour disturbances and general grumpiness than the older ones.

Third, severely epileptic children frequently have emotional problems for fairly obvious reasons – their lives have often been rather badly upset by the occurrence of convulsions; there may be stupid prejudice at school or elsewhere, and they and their families may be in a state of some tension as a result.

If you have a child with epilepsy and he is going through a hyperactive phase, you will know how trying it can be. Your paediatrician or neurologist may feel that it would be helpful to change his drugs and see what effect this has on his behaviour, but on no account should you stop the drugs of your own accord, since this will probably lead to a recurrence of fits. Do remember that there may be an emotional component in your child's hyperactivity. He needs a lot of love, reassurance and understanding. And try to bear in mind that phases of hyperactivity in epileptic children are just phases – it won't last for ever.

Children with emotional or psychological problems are often hyperactive. This is their way of seeking love and attention. By dashing around, knocking things over, breaking things, falling down (and raising the roof with crying) they are saying, 'Please, please look at me! Please love me!'

Unfortunately, they do it in such a way as to challenge the parent – to invite him to get cross or to lash out. When parents respond to this challenge, the poor disturbed child can at least say to himself, 'I was right! They don't love me!'

Dealing with this situation needs considerable skill and insight. By insight, I mean that the parents have to look carefully at themselves and at their own home situation; almost invariably, when a child starts behaving oddly there is something disturbing him at home.

If you cannot manage to sort the problem out for yourself, then talk to your GP, who may well be able to help you. He may call in a social worker to give advice. If necessary, he will refer you and your child to the department of child psychology at the nearest large hospital.

As you can see the problem of hyperactivity is usually rather complex. Finding the answer will frequently require a good deal of common sense and adaptability from both mother and father. The answer will not be found (as so many people imagine) by just going to the doctor to get something to quieten him down. Drugs of this kind are unlikely to help; they don't get at the root of the problem and may even make the child worse.

In recent years, there's been increasing interest – particularly among clinical ecologists – in the idea that some cases of hyperactivity may be due to food allergy.

I have to say that there is as yet no definite proof of this theory. But many parents – especially those associated with The Hyperactive Children's Support Group mentioned below – believe firmly that it's so. Many claim that their hyperactive children's behaviour has improved greatly as soon as certain items have been removed from their diet.

What items? Chemical food additives have not infrequently been incriminated, and there seems to be particular suspicion about the very common yellow food dye called tartrazine (you'll see it called E102 on packets).

In order to avoid these food additives and dyes, many parents of hyperactive children try the well-known exclusion diet called the Feingold diet (or the KP diet). If this doesn't work, it may perhaps be worth trying a diet which excludes other types of food (e.g. cow's milk) to which the child may be sensitive.

More details about exclusion diets are available from an excellent self-help group which now has over 150 branches in the UK (and that shows how common hyperactivity is!).

Write to them (enclosing an sae) at:

Hyperactive Children's Support
  Group
59 Meadowside
Angmering
West Sussex
BN16 4BW

HYPNOTISM

Hypnotism isn't used all that much in childhood illnesses, but may sometimes be helpful in treating spasms and habit tics, and also for snoring!

You should make sure you take your child to a medically qualified hypnotist (i.e. a doctor) rather than somebody who just advertises in the local paper.

Your GP may know of a qualified man or woman who does hypnosis. If not, then write to:

The British Society of
  Hypnotherapists
51 Queen Anne Street
London W1M 9FA

HYSTERIA

This is a state – common in older children (girls more than boys) – in which the child produces symptoms which have no physical cause. In other words, the symptom – which is frequently dramatic and sometimes bizarre – is due to emotional causes.

This *doesn't* mean the youngster is making it up or pretending – she isn't. In most cases, she believes fervently in the genuineness of her symptoms, and may be scared stiff by them. Common hysterical symptoms are sudden inexplicable blindness, paralysis, inability to speak, loss of consciousness, and so on.

In some cases, an important factor may be over-breathing (hyperventilation). It's not generally realized that if a child (or adult) gets a bit het up and starts breathing too fast, this rapid breathing may have a disorientating effect on the brain – because it 'washes out' too much carbon dioxide from the body.

For this reason, the simple procedure of getting an over-excited, hysterical child to breathe into a paper bag (which builds up the body's carbon dioxide again) is sometimes dramatically successful.

But in the long term, the treatment of recurrent hysteria involves prolonged psychotherapy and possibly family therapy too.

Mass hysteria (group hysteria) is surprisingly common in childhood, and major outbreaks of it occur every few years in Britain.

Typically, what happens is that large groups of children start collapsing at some public event at which they're under stress. (The drum-majorette parade is a classic case.) Newspaper headlines then suggest that the mass collapses are due to gas, or mystery viruses or food poisoning. (An ice-cream man was nearly beaten up by angry parents in one recent episode!)

These headlines then lead to further episodes of mass collapse in schools and children's organizations across the country. These 'outbreaks' lead to more flaming headlines, and to dramatic reports on TV news. As a result, more children start collapsing . . .

And so it goes on for a week or two, until everybody (the media included) starts behaving more sensibly and the whole thing is forgotten for a few years.

IMMUNIZATION

Every child should have the protection of all the available immunizations unless there's some good reason why not (see below).

Unfortunately, vast numbers of kids miss out on these vaccinations – partly because of understandable fears about the whooping cough jab. Mothers and fathers may decide not to bother with the other jabs – perhaps because they don't want to argue with the doctor about the whooping cough vaccination.

Remember that you can always refuse the whooping cough jab if you feel strongly – but let your child have the others.

So what vaccinations are now available for children in this country? The schedule which is put out by the Department of Health provides for immunization against diphtheria, whooping cough, tetanus (lockjaw), polio, measles, German measles, and TB.

The Schedule

There are seven immunizations in the official schedule (see below). Do bear in mind that, though this schedule is put out by a British government department

Age First year of life	Immunization	Notes
3 months	first polio drops first triple jab – diphtheria, tetanus (lockjaw) and whooping cough	If you don't want the whooping cough component, a double jab (diphtheria and tetanus only) is available
4½–5 months	second polio drops second triple jab	
8½–11 months	third polio drops third triple jab	
12 months	Measles jab	
School entry age	Booster polio drops Booster double jab (diphtheria and tetanus)	
Age 11 to 13	BCG (anti-TB) immunization	Given to Mantoux-negative children (see text)
	Girls: German measles (rubella) jab	Not at the same time as BCG
School-leaving age	Booster polio drops Booster tetanus jab	These two rarely seem to get done, unfortunately

and is therefore widely followed in many Commonwealth countries, your doctor isn't obliged by law to follow it. If she feels that in your child's particular case a jab should be given at a rather different time from that suggested on the schedule, then that's quite OK.

Diphtheria   The diphtheria vaccine is part of the famous triple jab which (as you can see from the schedule) is started early in the first year of life.

If you don't want the triple jabs because of the whooping cough component (see below) then ask your GP or clinic for the double jab, which only contains diphtheria and tetanus. Your child should quite definitely be protected against diphtheria. This disease killed thousands of children until only a generation ago, and the germs that cause it are still very much around. Deaths are very few these days – but if we don't keep up our children's protection against diphtheria, this hideous, choking killer will definitely come back.

Tetanus (lockjaw)   Tetanus is the extremely serious disease which you develop when lockjaw germs get into a cut. These germs are all over the place (particularly on roads and in soil) and they're always going to be with us. Tetanus deaths still occur, so obviously everybody ought to be fully protected against the disease.

Your child's protection comes from these three triple jabs (see schedule) plus the boosters at five and at school-leaving age. If you don't want the whooping cough part of the triple jab, then don't avoid immunizations altogether, but ask for the double jab which contains tetanus and diphtheria vaccines only.

Whooping cough   This is the immunization that all the row is about. It forms the third part of the triple jab, along with diphtheria and tetanus.

The trouble is that a very small number of children seem to have developed serious brain damage after being given whooping cough vaccine – though some medical authorities deny this altogether. Brain damage is a dreadful catastrophe for these poor children and their parents, but opinions differ as to whether these rare tragedies occur with sufficient frequency to make us abandon the whooping cough vaccination programme. Most doctors think it should be continued – especially after the whooping cough outbreaks which have occurred in recent years.

But some paediatricians feel that whooping cough is now a milder disease than it used to be. It's certainly a great trial to a child (and his parents) when he gets it, and it can be very serious – but it's rarely life-threatening in the way that it would have been, say, thirty years ago. Whooping cough deaths are now rare (roughly one case in 5000) and this may be due partly to the fact that the whooping cough germ has somehow changed its nature and become less dangerous.

However, the British government's official view at present is that routine vaccination against whooping cough should continue, especially as some whooping cough deaths have occurred since so many parents stopped having their children immunized against the disease. I think I should point out that many of these deaths have been among babies who were too young to be immunized anyway.

On the other hand, it's true that very young babies' lives would be saved if there weren't so much whooping cough around: in other words, we protect young babies by immunizing older ones.

Your baby should probably not have the whooping cough component of the triple vaccine in three circumstances:

- if he has had convulsions in the past
- if he has previously had some kind of 'funny' reaction to a triple jab
- if there is a very strong family history of convulsions.

There's also doubt as to whether a child who has had a very difficult birth should have the whooping cough jab.

Clearly, you'll need to talk all this over with your doctor or clinic. But *don't* abandon all vaccinations because you're worried about the whooping cough one.

Polio You may not be old enough to remember it yourself, but polio killed or paralysed thousands upon thousands of children (and adults) until the late 1950s when vaccination against it became nearly universal. Such tragedies are rare today.

But polio germs are still around, and as I've explained, the disease will come back if we don't keep up our guard. Rather worryingly, polio is the immunization that people seem to forget most easily, particularly when going abroad to countries (like those of North Africa) where polio viruses are rampant. Perhaps this immunization gets forgotten because it's so easily given – not by a jab these days, but by three drops of fluid, taken by mouth.

Your child should have his first three lots of polio drops (on a lump of sugar or just dropped on to his tongue) at the same time as his three triple jabs (see schedule). Boosters should be given at five, at school leaving, and if he travels to anywhere outside Europe – also if he goes to Holland, where there have been outbreaks in recent years because of religious opposition to vaccination.

BCG This is the anti-TB vaccine which has made such a contribution to conquering tuberculosis all over the world. In Britain, children from about the age of ten onwards are given skin tests to determine their susceptibility to TB. Those who are tuberculin-negative (that is, susceptible to TB) are offered the vaccination. At the time of writing, there's a proposal to drop routine BCG immunization, and only give it to selected children.

Until quite recently, most children came into contact with TB germs in early life and with luck developed at least some natural immunity against the disease and didn't need BCG. But these days, there's relatively little TB around.

BCG isn't given by injection, so there's no real jab. It's pricked through the skin of the upper arm with a special instrument and this is virtually painless.

German measles German measles (rubella) is usually a mild illness, but if a pregnant woman gets it the effects on her unborn baby can be truly terrible.

So, in Britain, all girls are offered German measles vaccination between the ages of eleven and thirteen. (In the USA, boys are offered it as well.) Don't turn the offer down because you think that your daughter has had German measles already – you may well be quite wrong! Careful studies involving blood tests have shown that a very large percentage of girls who have been diagnosed as suffering from German measles in the past must in fact have had some other infection instead. So *all* girls should have this jab.

Holiday immunizations

Every year, some children come home with serious infections which they've picked up abroad. So take your youngster to your GP at least a couple of months before your holiday and get those immunizations up to date.

Nowadays, most GPs have a regularly updated list of which jabs are needed for which country. If there's any doubt (particularly if there's some controversy over whether a vaccination is necessary), a most reliable source of information is the British Airways medical department (they can also do the jabs, for a small fee).

What are the important diseases you should consider?

Polio   Above all, *don't* forget polio. If there's one immunization which your child (and yourself) should be up-to-date with before he goes abroad, this is it. Remember that the polio vaccine isn't given by injection. There's no need even for a jab – just three drops of liquid by mouth, usually on a lump of sugar.

Smallpox   Since 1979, there has been no danger anywhere of this disease, either for children or for adults. Since smallpox vaccination carries a small element of risk, there's no point in your family having it.

One or two states still insist on your having it (thinking that they're protecting themselves) and, until they wake up to the fact that it is no longer a danger, you'll have to go along with them and have it done before you go there.

Cholera   This has spread in the most worrying fashion in recent years, and

several cases reached Britain in the mid-1980s. There have been outbreaks in Portugal, Italy and other Mediterranean countries over the last few summers. The only continents which have remained immune at the time of writing are Australasia and the Americas. Cholera spread to southern Africa for the first time a few years ago, and is now a threat in much of the African continent.

So you and your children need this jab if you're going to most countries of the world – particularly those of Asia and Africa. The jab lasts six months.

Typhoid   This disease used at one time to be common even in the cool north of France, but it isn't now. Whether it's worth having the injection if you're going to the southern part of France is arguable. Many people don't because the jab so often makes a child – and even an adult – feel really rotten, with a very sore arm.

For Portugal, Spain and Italy, the case for having the jab is rather stronger – and for North Africa or anywhere in the tropics it's absolutely vital. The jab lasts three years.

Yellow fever   Not needed unless you're going to West Africa, or South or Central America. This is the one injection you can't get from your GP: you have to go to a special yellow fever immunization centre. Your doctor or local Public Health Department will give you the address of the nearest one. The jab lasts ten years.

Certificates   Whoever immunizes you and your children – whether it's your GP or the British Airways medical centre or a yellow fever centre, will issue you a signed and stamped certificate to show to authorities in the countries you travel to (if they want to see it). Note that your GP is entitled to make a modest charge for this certificate.

Malaria There is no immunization against malaria, though parents taking a child to a hot country often ask for one.

Protection comes in the form of anti-malaria tablets, which need to be taken (by both children and yourself) from before you go away until after you come back.

Your GP will prescribe these tablets for you, if you're going to a tropical country. Incidentally, they're not supposed to be on the NHS, so you'll have to pay the chemist – however, the common forms of anti-malaria tablet are incredibly cheap when one considers the terrible harm malaria can do to your child – or yourself.

IMPETIGO

This common childhood skin infection is caused by the staphylococcus germ – the one which you find in boils and styes.

It causes a little golden, crusty blistery eruption on the child's skin – most often on his face. It seems to be spread by direct contact – which is why, in Rugby-playing schools, it's often ruefully referred to as 'scrumpox'!

Impetigo isn't serious, and these days is quickly cleared up with antibiotic cream (and possibly medicine).

In the meantime, don't touch the rash – except to apply the cream. Wash your hands immediately afterwards. Don't let your child touch the area – it's infectious! And keep him away from school till the doctor says he can go back.

INDIGESTION

This isn't often much of a problem in childhood, though some children do get problems with heartburn-type pains.

The best thing to do is not to make a fuss about it, because it's not going to lead to anything serious. Give the child a glass of milk when the feeling comes on. If this doesn't work, any mild proprietary antacid (e.g. Rennies) should do the trick.

INFANTILE PARALYSIS

See *Polio* and *Immunization*.

INFECTIOUS HEPATITIS

See *Jaundice*.

INFECTIOUS MONONUCLEOSIS

See *Glandular fever*.

INFLUENZA

'Flu isn't usually a life-threatening illness in a child (as it is in old people) but it can make her feel extremely miserable. It's important to get medical help, because there is a small risk of complications such as pneumonia or ear ache.

'Flu is caused by a virus, and influenza viruses go swooping round the world in quite dramatic outbreaks. So, usually, the newspapers or TV news will have alerted you to the fact that there's a lot of 'flu around.

Symptoms of 'flu may include:

- 'coldy' symptoms – sneezing, etc
- severe aches and pains all over
- high temperature
- weakness
- in a minority of cases, diarrhoea or vomiting.

If you suspect 'flu, keep the child at home (*don't* go down to the surgery) and phone the doctor. She may or may not prescribe antibiotics – doctors differ a bit on this one. Antibiotics have absolutely no effect whatever on the 'flu virus, but some GPs think it's worth giving them in case the child gets a secondary infection (which is common) with germs that *do* respond to antibiotics.

Otherwise, the doctor will just suggest paracetamol, plus plenty of fluids – and bed rest till the patient feels better.

Usually the illness will be over in about four days – so contact the doctor again if the child doesn't improve or if her condition inexplicably takes a turn for the worse. (See *Reye's syndrome*.)

Immunization

There are vaccines against 'flu, but it's not official Government policy to give them routinely to children. The vaccines offer only limited protection because of the 'flu virus's amazing ability to change its nature every few months or so.

The manufacturers of these vaccines tend to suggest that everyone should have the vaccine. Many big firms do the same, in an understandable bid to protect their work forces! Your doctor may be willing to vaccinate your child each winter if you wish, but she'll probably point out that the vaccine carries a small

risk of side-effects. In practice, few parents have their kids immunized.

INGROWING TOENAIL

Vast numbers of children get ingrowing big toenails, probably because of shoes that fit too tightly. (My own ingrowing toenail was very likely due to a heavy weighing machine falling on my foot at the age of two!)

If you discover that your child has an ingrowing toenail, what do you do? Nearly all popular medical books say that you should cut a V in the middle of the child's nail, and that this will somehow make it grow straight.

Nowadays chiropodists reckon that this is nonsense! In fact, the best thing is to cut the nail straight across, as shown in the picture opposite. Try not to dig down into the corners.

If the nail is causing any pain, it's best to take the child to a chiropodist. Chiropodists really are the most skilled people at dealing with nails, and the deft way in which they can cut back a nail so as to relieve pain is really most impressive.

In severe cases, your GP will probably want to send the child to hospital to have a small operation. In my view, you should agree to this *only* if the doctor sends your child to an orthopaedic surgeon. To be frank, I've seen too many children's toenails which have been hacked about by enthusiastic young casualty officers!

If the skin alongside the ingrowing toenail becomes red and infected, take the youngster to your doctor, because this is probably a whitlow (see *Whitlow*).

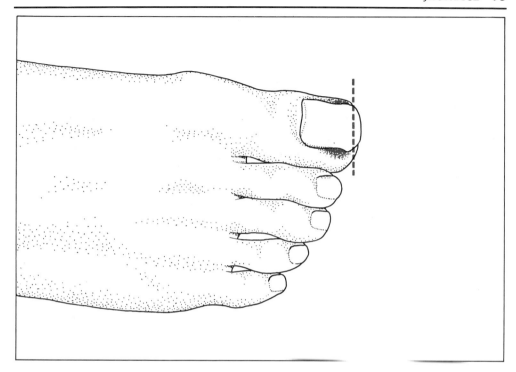

INTUSSUSCEPTION

This is a 'telescoping' of the child's bowel – in other words, when one part of it slides inside the next. It produces severe tummy ache, and often rectal bleeding, as well as blockage of the bowels.

Intussusception is most common round about the time a baby is weaned, and it could be that sometimes it's the introduction of solid food that sparks it off.

In the old days, intussusception could be fatal, but today prompt intervention by a surgeon will cure the problem. The surgeon will arrange a barium enema – a special x-ray in which dye is injected into the rectum to find out the exact site of the blockage. Sometimes, the enema itself actually unblocks the bowel. But if this doesn't happen, the surgeon will go ahead and operate. The results of the operation are very good.

JAUNDICE

This is a yellowness of the child's skin and eyes, due to a build-up of yellow bile pigment.

There are literally dozens of possible causes of jaundice in childhood. Fortunately, the outlook in most cases is good. Here's a list of the more common causes:

Newborn

Jaundice of prematurity   Common in premature babies. Usually fades after a few days.

Jaundice caused by Rhesus factor   Increasingly rare these days, because vulnerable women are given a protective injection. But if it occurs, the blood bile pigment level can go so high that it may harm the child's brain. If there's any risk of this, the hospital will do an exchange transfusion, to give the baby what is virtually a complete change of blood.

Toddlers and Schoolchildren

Infectious hepatitis (infective jaundice) This still affects several hundred British children every year. The cause is a virus which affects the liver. The child usually becomes ill about six weeks after exposure to the virus.

The main treatment is bedrest and abstention from alcohol (*not* a major consideration in many toddlers' lives!).

Nearly all children recover completely in about a month or so, though a very small proportion do develop more serious liver disease.

Some doctors believe that children who have this type of jaundice should have a special diet, in which fatty foods are restricted. Others don't believe that there's any point in this. There's certainly no point at all in giving antibiotics, as these have no effect on the virus.

KNOCK KNEES

Mild knock knees are still sometimes seen, especially in children with flat feet, though it doesn't seem to be as common as it used to be. In mild cases no treatment may be required. If you're worried about your child's appearance, however, your orthopaedic surgeon may decide to prescribe small wedges which will go under the inner side of her foot – or just possibly splints.

In severe cases, an operation can be carried out to straighten the leg.

However, many children do grow out of a knock-kneed appearance, especially if this is due to carrying too much bodyweight early in life.

LEAD POISONING

In the days when the paint on children's cots contained lead, this used to be common. If your child has a very old-fashioned cot, you should certainly stop him from nibbling the paint, just in case!

A greater danger these days is that the child may breathe in lead from dust or fumes, particularly if he lives near a lead factory or if his parents work in the lead industry and bring dust home on their clothes.

Symptoms of lead poisoning include colicky pain, anaemia, weakness and mental impairment.

The diagnosis is made by a blood test, and treatment is with a drug which helps to clear lead from the body.

LEUKAEMIA

Leukaemia is one of the most frightening of childhood illnesses, and many parents dread the possibility of this blood disorder striking their child.

However, the outlook is nowhere as bleak as it used to be a few years ago, and if a child gets leukaemia (particularly what is called the acute lymphatic form) there is now a very good chance that he can be cured.

Leukaemia is a cancer of the white blood cells. Blood contains two main types of cell – red and white. The white cells are concerned with important jobs such as mopping up germs that try to get into the body, and helping to maintain the child's immunity to infections.

These white cells are manufactured mainly in the bone marrow – which can be found inside many bones in our body. White cells are manufactured all the time, and in very great numbers, and the reason for this is that they are constantly being worn out by the various defensive jobs they have to do round the body.

A child's bone marrow, then, is a very busy factory, turning out white blood cells day and night – but at a rate which is just right to balance the wastage of cells which are being used up in the blood. This balance is very cleverly maintained by the body, and it is remarkable that when a child is in a state of good health, the number of white cells in his blood remains constant.

What happens in leukaemia is that something goes desperately wrong with the balance, and white cells start being produced in the most prodigious numbers. This over-production of cells is typical of cancers; in fact, that's what cancer really means: a sudden loss of control over the cells in some part of the body, so that they reproduce at frightening speed, producing masses and masses of cells that destroy everything else.

The leukaemic child's blood is full of white cells – and, unfortunately, these are very immature white cells which are no good at protecting the child against the germs to which he is exposed every day of his life.

As a result, within a very short time he has virtually no defence against infection. At the same time, the surfeit of abnormal white cells in his body makes him weak and run-down. There is usually an associated anaemia – that is, a lack of red cells – so that he's likely to look pale and wan.

The main features of leukaemia are great paleness, weakness, anaemia that does not respond to treatment, enlargement of the spleen and recurrent unexplained bleeding.

A doctor who notes these features will arrange a blood test that will often make the diagnosis clear. However, it's usually necessary to confirm the diagnosis, and make a better assessment of the situation by putting a needle into the child's bone marrow (in the chest or hip region) and sucking out some cells to look at under a microscope. This hurts a little bit, but most kids are very brave about it.

What causes leukaemia? Sadly the answer (as with so many diseases) is that we don't know. The origins of most forms of cancer are still shrouded in mystery (with the notable exception of lung cancer).

However, certain facts are known about the possible causes of leukaemia. It doesn't seem to be infectious in any way, because children don't catch it from each other. (In some ways, this is a bit surprising because it is known that leukaemia of cats can be passed from animal to animal.)

It doesn't seem to be hereditary, since there's no obvious tendency for leukaemia to run in families. However, there is much evidence that it can be caused by radiation. The survivors of Hiroshima and Nagasaki, for example, had a twentyfold increase in leukaemia. Patients who have had intensive radiotherapy for a long period of time also have an increased incidence of leukaemia. So, too, do doctors who work with x-rays.

An additional and rather disquieting fact is that the incidence of leukaemia throughout the world has been increasing very markedly over the last twenty years or so. Some of this could be just an apparent increase, due to improved methods of diagnosis of leukaemia, but the rise in leukaemia deaths in Britain throughout the 1960s was very worrying and I feel that it's possible that it may have been due to the increased radiation caused by H-bomb testing.

But I'm very pleased to say that in the last few years, leukaemia deaths in Britain have actually levelled out – and it may be that this is related to the fact that there have been far less H-bomb explosions since the nuclear test ban treaty of the 1960s. However, I must stress that this is just guesswork at the moment.

Until very recently there was almost no hope for either a child or an adult with leukaemia. Drugs could be given which would damp down the activity of the rapidly multiplying cells in the bone marrow, and transfusions administered in order to combat the severe anaemia, but the end result was always the same. As recently as 1975, a distinguished paediatrician wrote with complete accuracy: 'there is as yet no cure for leukaemia.'

Since then things have moved very fast. By 1977, doctors working in the field of leukaemia therapy were confident that they had, at last, been able to save the lives of a small proportion of the children who had been referred to them with this dreaded disease. Today, some children have a better than even chance of a cure.

No one, of course, can ever be *sure* that a disease of this sort is really cured until a child has been totally free of symptoms for many years. But at the present moment, the indications are good, and it does seem that a good many British children have had leukaemia, have been treated, and are now totally free of any sign of the disease.

The treatment varies depending on which type of leukaemia the child has but, normally, it includes a combination of drugs which destroy the abnormal white cells and stop the marrow cells from producing more. Choosing the right combination of drugs, and knowing at what intervals to give them is a very precise and complex business.

In addition, a most important development of recent years has been the use of x-rays to destroy the abnormal cells. The x-rays are administered to the child's brain area (into which the drugs are not very good at penetrating) and the use of this therapy does seem to be associated with a much better survival rate.

Of course, the therapy is not without problems: it's a drastic form of treatment and the child often feels ill during it. His hair frequently falls out (though only temporarily) and he has to be in hospital and to some extent separated from his family, which is upsetting for him.

If, however, the treatment is successfully completed, there's now a reasonable chance that he will be completely better after it, so it's certainly well worth having. Admittedly, the psychological stresses on him – and on his parents – are very considerable, and not all families can cope with the strain.

However, any reader of this book

who has a leukaemic child in the family should take heart. The chances of success are now better than they've ever been, and the advances in leukaemia therapy of the last few years have been remarkable. Long may they continue.

LICE

See *Nits*.

LOCKJAW *(Tetanus)*

This very serious infection is caused by germs which are found in soil and in gravel and on road surfaces. The germs get into cuts (particularly deep ones) and produce a chemical which paralyses the child's muscles, and may kill him.

Some parents are convinced that lockjaw is caused by rust (e.g. on nails), but this definitely isn't so.

Thank Heavens, tetanus is now pretty rare in Britain, because of the very effective immunization which is used against it. Every child should have this immunization – which is given as part of the double or triple jab (see *Immunization*), which is usually started when a child is about three months old.

But (and it's a big but) if your child sustains a deep or dirty cut – particularly one contaminated by soil – always wash it very carefully and then take him to a doctor or an accident department. Even though he has had his jabs, an additional anti-lockjaw injection may still be necessary.

MEASLES

This virus infection affects about one in six of all British kids. This is quite unnecessary, as there's a perfectly good jab which will prevent measles and its possible serious complications.

The measles virus is passed from one child's mouth or nose to another's. Even quite brief contact is enough to cause infection – for instance, a short chat between your child and another who's in the process of developing the illness will ensure that your youngster has spots in store (unless, of course, he's been vaccinated against measles).

When the virus has entered your child's mouth or nose, there's an interval of about ten days or so before anything happens.

At the end of this incubation period, he'll get what seems to be just a cold, with the usual symptoms, such as runny nose and so on. But one thing that might make you suspicious is that the child usually has very runny eyes. He may also say that the light hurts his eyes.

It's about another four days before he gets the spots, and unfortunately, it's during this period that he's at his most infectious, and may give the virus to half a dozen of his mates.

The rash usually starts behind the ears, and then spreads across the face, and develops on the whole body (see picture overleaf). It's a brownish-red, almost coppery rash, in which the spots sort of merge with each other. There are no pustules or blobs of fluid.

There's often an early clue inside the mouth to the diagnosis – an inside rash composed of little pinhead-sized bumps called Koplik's spots. Sometimes your

GP can detect measles before the skin rash has come out, by finding these tell-tale spots.

More often, your youngster has had the skin rash for at least a day – and has spread the virus before anybody realizes what's happening.

If you find a rash which you think may be due to measles on your child, keep him at home. Don't send him to school or playschool with the idea of waiting and seeing – he'll only give it to other children. Also, as with other rashes, you shouldn't take the child to your GP's and sit him in the waiting-room.

It's best to keep the child at home, phone your GP and describe the symptoms. He may visit you, or he may arrange for you to bring the child down when surgery is over. (As long as you can bring him by car, this will do him no harm.)

Assuming that your GP says that it *is* measles, and not some other rash-producing illness (of which there are many), you should have the child at home for at least a week. Your doctor will advise you how soon he can go back to school or playschool, depending on how fast he's recovering.

Meantime, his friends must stay away from the house, unless they've had the measles jab. It's usually too late as far as brothers and sisters are concerned!

Therefore, the only treatment is to keep the child in bed for a couple of days, and then let him get up and play around the house. He should drink lots of liquid (ice-cold squash is good), but don't press him to eat unless he really feels like it. If your youngster gets some secondary infection (say, a bad cough following close on the measles) antibiotics will be needed.

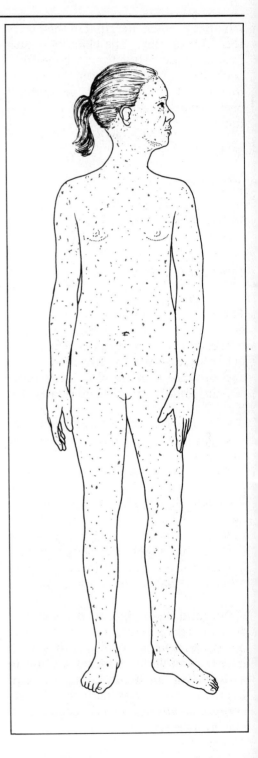

Complications of measles are uncommon, but can be serious – which is why a jab against the disease has been developed. They include brain inflammation and ear trouble. Also, kids can get nasty chest infections – so if your youngster is coughing a lot at the same time, ring the doctor.

I'm sure you'll see from this list of complications that no child should ever be deliberately exposed to measles (a practice that some parents still believe in). Immunization is far safer.

Because of the risk of these complications, nearly all toddlers should have the measles jab when they're aged one. It's very regrettable that at the moment, most parents *aren't* getting their youngsters 'done'. Measles is preventable – but it's up to you to prevent it.

Alternative treatment
Naturopaths tend to suggest fasting and hydrotherapy. **Homoeopaths** suggest pulsatilla, aconite, and what is claimed to be a specific anti-measles treatment called 'Morbillimum 200'.

MENINGITIS

This very serious infection of the membranes which cover the child's brain is caused by a germ, usually breathed in from a person who's a healthy carrier of it.

Fortunately, meningitis is quite rare, with only a few hundred cases occurring each year (though mini-outbreaks have occurred in Gloucestershire and one or two other areas in recent years).

Regrettably, the very rareness of meningitis makes it quite difficult for doctors to diagnose. I recently calcu-

lated that the average GP would see a case only once in about sixty years!

So the danger of meningitis is that it may go unrecognized until it's too late.

Symptoms to look out for are:
- severe headache
- stiffness of the neck
- dislike of the light
- raised temperature
- confusion
- sometimes, a purplish rash.

If you ever suspect meningitis in your child, ring your doctor and tell her why you're worried. If the doctor's examination suggests that meningitis is a possibility, she'll admit the child to hospital, where a test called a lumbar puncture will almost certainly be done. This involves tapping off some fluid from the spine.

The test makes clear whether meningitis is present, and indicates exactly which germs are responsible – and to which antibiotics they'll respond. If the course of antibiotics is started promptly, there's an excellent chance of the child's swift and complete recovery.

MIGRAINE

This common condition is believed to be caused by an odd reaction to certain stimuli in the arteries (blood-carrying tubes) inside the skull.

The most usual symptom is severe headache, which is usually felt only on one side of the head. The headache is often preceded by odd visual disturbances – for instance, a sensation of dazzling lights or zig-zag lines.

Soon after the attack starts, the child often vomits. Naturally, this causes an extra problem, in that any anti-migraine tablets given to him may well not be absorbed.

It's not clear why some children should get migraine, while others don't. There seems to be a marked family tendency, so probably there's a hereditary factor which makes the arteries in the skull react in this odd way to certain provoking factors.

Stress – including exam stress – may be one such factor. Chocolate, oranges and Chianti (not imbibed by many kids, fortunately!) have been known for many years to trigger off migraine attacks in some people.

When your child gets an attack of migraine, proceed as follows:

1   lie him down in a darkened room;
2   give him paracetamol as soon as possible (before the migraine upsets his stomach and interferes with the absorption of the pills);
3   if your doctor has suggested a 'stomach-settling' drug, such as metoclopramide, give it as early as possible in the attack; with luck, this will ensure that the paracetamol is absorbed;
4   put a bucket or potty by the bed, in case he's sick;
5   let the child go to sleep if he wants to. In most cases, he'll feel much better after a brief doze.

Some doctors give migrainous children the powerful drug ergotamine. This can be of value, but you should be very careful about how you use it. Many parents don't realize that excessive use of this drug can actually give the child headaches, rather than relieve them.

Finally, when things are bad, do try and remember that many children do eventually grow out of this trying disorder.

Alternative therapy

Herbalists tend to recommend the plant feverfew – which is now being used very widely by parents. But do be careful with the dose, which isn't easy to gauge.

Clinical ecologists quite rightly lay considerable stress on trying to find out which items in the child's diet may provoke attacks. They maintain that in addition to chocolate and oranges (mentioned above), tea, wheat derivatives, artificial colours, eggs and lemons may be responsible.

MONGOLISM

This is now referred to as Down's syndrome. See *Down's syndrome*

MUCOVISCIDOSIS

See *Cystic fibrosis*.

MUMPS (*Parotitis*)

This common childhood infection is caused by a virus which is breathed out by another infected person. Mini-epidemics occur in schools and play-schools quite frequently.

The incubation period of mumps is quite long – usually about eighteen to twenty-eight days. At the end of this time, the child becomes generally off-colour, loses her appetite and develops a temperature.

One or both cheeks then start to swell up. This is because the virus has affected the two big saliva glands (the parotids) which lie in front of the child's ear.

Unfortunately, this swelling causes the child quite a bit of pain, especially when she tries to eat. In fact, she may have several quite miserable days ahead of her, I'm afraid.

If you suspect that your child has mumps, don't take her down to the doctor's surgery. Put her to bed and ask your GP to call. If he confirms the diagnosis, there's no medicine he can give to cure her. The mumps virus doesn't respond to antibiotics, so there's no point in giving them.

All you can do is make the child comfortable in bed for a few days. Most importantly, give her lots of cool drinks instead of solid food, so that she doesn't have to chew. Liquidizing food may be helpful, and she may prefer to suck it through a straw.

Paracetamol will make her feel a bit better and relieve the pain. A wrapped-up hotty on the cheek may sometimes help.

With luck the child should be better and back at playschool or school within about ten days – be guided by your doctor.

Very occasionally children do get complications of mumps. These may include painful inflammation of the ovaries or testicles, and (most uncommonly) inflammation of the brain. If your youngster seems strangely drowsy and clearly isn't recovering from the mumps, contact your doctor immediately.

Fathers and older brothers are at some small risk of developing painful and potentially harmful inflammation of the testicles if they catch mumps from the child. So if they haven't already had

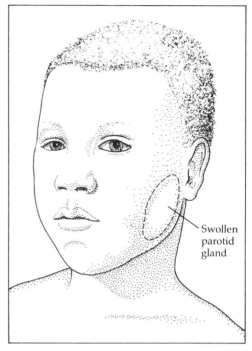

Swollen parotid gland

mumps, it's probably a good idea for them to avoid very close physical contact with an infected child.

There is a vaccine against mumps, but it's not part of the routine schedule in Britain. However, it can be arranged by a doctor if an outbreak occurs in a boarding school or other institution.

Alternative therapy
Homoeopathic doctors use aconite, sulphur and the appropriately named 'parotidinum' to treat mumps.

NAPPY RASH

Nappy rash is enough to drive any mother round the bend! It can drag on in the most infuriating way. And I have to admit that some mothers don't feel that the health professionals seem to be taking it seriously enough.

But the two important things to remember about nappy rash are:

- bad as it may look to you, it *isn't* a serious disease, and often doesn't trouble the baby anything like as much as it worries the parents
- it will always get better in the end (sorry!).

In fact, with determined efforts by mother plus doctor plus (if necessary) the health visitor or nurse, nappy rash can often be defeated very quickly. But it's unlikely to be defeated just by the use of some magic drug or application, as parents often think.

Why not? Well, the reason is very simple. Nappy rash is caused by nappies – and by plastic pants. That's why babies born in countries where children run around with no clothes on don't get nappy rash.

Therefore, very often the best treatment of nappy rash is to expose the child's bottom. Certainly, in all cases, you should stop using plastic pants until the child is completely better. This is the most difficult point for doctors to get over to many parents – understandably, of course, because it's Mum (and not the doctor) who has to clear up the mess caused by a baby not wearing plastic pants!

In most cases, nappy rash occurs because the urine in the baby's wet nappy is in contact with the child's skin for too long. Germs break down chemicals in this urine to form ammonia – a strong irritant to the baby's skin.

Since the ammonia can't evaporate (because of the plastic pants), it attacks the poor old baby's bottom – causing a red and/or spotty rash.

If you notice that a nappy rash is appearing, take the following action:

1 stop using plastic pants
2 wherever possible, let the child go without nappies, and let the sun and air get to her bottom (yes, I know it's difficult)
3 after any soiling wash baby's bottom thoroughly, dry it gently, and then apply a proprietary barrier cream or just plain traditional old zinc oxide cream, to protect the baby's skin against further attack by ammonia
4 when the baby *does* have to have a nappy on, use one-way disposable liners, which help to keep her skin dry.

If these measures don't work, you'll have to seek expert professional help. The doctor or the health visitor may decide that the baby has one or other of these additional problems:

Infection   often with that well-known fungus called thrush. For this, an anti-fungus cream will be prescribed (see *Thrush*).

Allergic skin reaction   see *Eczema*. This may be a reaction to chemicals in the detergent or conditioner (or possibly to some application which has been put on the bottom) – the treatment is to try and avoid the irritant chemical, and also to apply an anti-inflammatory cream which will be prescribed by your doctor.

Nappy rash is for some reason rather less common in breast-fed babies – so you can help to avoid it at birth by starting your baby on the breast rather than the bottle.

NATUROPATHY

This system of alternative medicine relies on the body's ability to heal itself, given the right conditions.

Naturopathy has become increasingly popular in recent years, partly because its practitioners don't give strong drugs – which therefore don't cause the all too frequent side-effects which are associated with the medicine prescribed by us orthodox doctors.

Instead, naturopaths tend to try to treat illness by fasting, diet modification (including avoidance of refined sugar), meditation and relaxation. For obvious reasons, some of these techniques are very difficult to use on children! Many British naturopaths are also qualified in osteopathy (see *Osteopathy*) and use this in their work.

Because naturopathy seems to be a pretty harmless way of treating people, it isn't regarded with any great amount of hostility by orthodox doctors. But I think you should be wary of allowing purely naturopathic treatment on your child in cases of serious disease. (Personally, I'm a bit alarmed to see that one standard book on naturopathy says that some naturopaths will try and treat meningitis or pneumonia with naturopathic methods. This would be quite crazy – and extremely likely to lead to the death of the child.)

Another aspect of naturopathy which I find a bit worrying is the tendency to oppose all forms of childhood immunization. The same book which I've quoted above suggests to parents that they shouldn't even have their youngsters vaccinated against polio (see *Polio*). This seems to me to be the height of lunacy.

However, where non-life threatening disorders, behaviour problems and perhaps allergies are concerned, you are unlikely to do your child any harm at all by consulting a trained naturopath.

But do note that word trained. Anyone can call himself a naturopath – and lots of optimistic cowboys do! There are two well-established groups of trained naturopaths, about 250 in all and you can recognize their members by the way they describe themselves in telephone directories, etc.

Members of the British Naturopathic and Osteopathic Association, who have had a four-year training, put the initials MBNOA after their names. Members of the Incorporated Society of Registered Naturopaths put the description Registered Naturopath after the name.

NEPHRITIS

This is the name applied to several different kidney diseases. One is caused by a throat infection or tonsillitis, which the child had two or three weeks earlier. In other types, the cause is unknown.

Possible symptoms of nephritis include blood in the child's urine, and swelling of her face.

Fortunately, most children with nephritis do make a good recovery these days. In a few instances, the child goes into kidney failure, which used to be fatal in all cases. Nowadays, it can be successfully treated by putting the child on an artificial kidney, and (if it becomes necessary) by doing a kidney transplant.

NERVES AND NERVOUSNESS

See *Stress*.

NETTLE RASH

See *Urticaria*.

NIGHTMARES

Nearly all children get nightmares at some time – and very frightening they can be too.

Factors which can provoke them include:

- worry and emotional stress (see *Stress*)
- seeing frightening films or TV programmes
- being under the weather with a feverish illness.

The time-honoured belief that certain foods (e.g. cheese) can produce nightmares doesn't seem to be true.

If your child just has an occasional nightmare, then there's no need to worry. When she wakes up frightened, or stumbles terrified into your bedroom in the middle of the night, just give her a big cuddle and explain to her that everything's all right.

But if nightmares are really persistent and are causing a lot of distress, you need to do something about it. Begin by asking yourself whether its due to any trouble at home or at school. (Is it, for instance, just the arrival of a new baby which has unsettled your child?)

If this commonsense measure fails, then talk things over with your doctor. If she can't put her finger on anything, then it may be necessary to consult a psychologist or a child psychiatrist – especially if there's a strong symbolic clement to the nightmares.

NITS

To nearly everybody, the word nits means head lice – though strictly speaking, the word originally meant the tiny white eggs of these little beasties.

To many parents this is an embarrassing subject and they are very reluctant even to admit the possibility that their youngsters might have nits.

But in large areas of the country, most schoolkids have had or will have nits. They are nothing to be ashamed of! Your child can't help getting them – and there's no way you can prevent him from getting them.

The head louse is a tiny creature which is only distantly related to the other types of louse (the body louse and the pubic louse); it affects only the hair, and never goes for other parts of the body.

While on the head, it does nothing very much except taking an occasional bite out of the scalp and, from time to time, laying little white eggs which stick to the base of your child's hair.

Since all children touch heads with each other at school – dozens of times a day, in fact – it's dead easy for the louse to walk from one child's head to another, and indeed to step daintily from your youngster's head on to yours. So when your child does get nits, the whole family must be treated.

You usually find out about head lice in one or two ways. First, you may well get a discreet phone call or note from the school nurse.

Second, you yourself may notice that your child can't stop scratching his scalp. Head louse bites are very itchy and produce an intolerable urge to scratch.

There are other causes of an itchy scalp, but these days the chances are it is the dreaded nits. If in the slightest doubt, take him down to your doctor and let him have a look. However, you yourself may be able to see the tiny creatures – and you'll almost certainly be able to detect the little white eggs stuck to the hairs, particularly if you use a fine-tooth comb.

Fortunately, once the initial shock of discovery is over, treatment is fairly easy. Your doctor can prescribe it for you, but in practice many mothers do just go and buy the necessary stuff over the counter from the chemist. (It's very cheap.) Don't be embarrassed about asking for it: they're only too delighted to flog it to you, since it's one of their best-selling lines!

Various treatments are available. You don't take anything by mouth: it's all done with applications to the scalp. These are the three main types:

- containing carbaryl (a relatively mild anti-nit agent): Carylderm lotion or shampoo; Derbac shampoo.
- containing malathion (a more powerful agent; be particularly careful to keep these preparations out of children's reach, and don't use them repeatedly without medical advice): Derbac liquid, Prioderm lotion or shampoo.
- containing gamma benzene hexachloride (again, take special care to keep these out of the children's reach): Esoderm shampoo, Lorexane No 3, Quellada Application PC in shampoo base.

All these potions are obtainable without prescription. But don't leave them lying around the house, and when using them take care to keep the stuff out of the eyes. (If any gets in, wash it out immediately with lots of water.)

It probably doesn't matter very much which preparation you pick, but on the whole your children are likely to prefer one of the shampoos, which can be washed out immediately, rather than lotions, which are very pongy and have to be left on all night.

The other thing you'll need if you're to defeat the head louse is a fine-tooth comb. This is to use after putting the application on the scalp. People tend not to bother about buying such a comb, because they think that applying a wonder drug to the scalp ought to be enough. But I would advise you to buy one and to use it on your family for a few days after treating their heads – otherwise you may get a relapse.

Fine-tooth combs can be bought very cheaply from chemists. If you can't face it, buy one at a pet shop and pretend it's for the cat.

NOSEBLEEDS

Nearly all children get nosebleeds from time to time – sometimes for no apparent reason; sometimes because of nose-picking or as a result of a bash on the nose.

Parents tend to worry about recurrent nosebleeds, fearing that they may be a sign of some serious disease, but this is only very rarely so.

Instead of lying the child down and sticking keys down her back, the correct procedure for nosebleeds is as follows:

1 sit the child up;
2 squeeze the soft part of her nose firmly between finger and thumb.

Keep the pressure up for at least ten minutes. Resist the temptation to relax the pressure and 'peek'! This is the most common reason for failure of treatment;

3   don't push cotton wool or anything else into the nostrils;

4   when the child has recovered, don't let her blow her nose for at least three hours.

In very rare cases, bleeding is uncontrollable by these means, and you'll have to take the child to an accident and emergency department.

Recurrent nosebleeds may be due to a weak blood vessel in the front of the nose. In these cases, an ear, nose and throat surgeon can 'cauterize' (i.e. 'fry') the blood vessel under local anaesthetic.

OBESITY

See *Fatness.*

OSTEOPATHY

Osteopathy is a form of alternative medicine which has gained tremendous acceptance (even among many doctors) in recent years. Its manipulation techniques have something in common with chiropractic (see *Chiropractic*).

Although osteopaths in some countries have quite irrationally tried to use manipulation to treat generalized illnesses, in Britain, most trained and qualified osteopaths use it mainly for spinal and bone troubles – which is fair enough.

But not all that many children go to osteopaths in the UK – mainly because very few children have spinal or bone problems. The one common spine problem (osteochondritis) does *not* respond well to manipulation, and good osteopaths will not try to treat it. (See also *Backache.*)

However, some specialized osteopaths do claim good results from treating children with back deformities, and even skull deformities. Others use manipulation to try to relieve the symptoms of childhood rheumatoid arthritis (see *Still's Disease*).

Warning. Anyone can call himself or herself an osteopath. An amazing number of persons with little or no training do just that. You should only take your child to a qualified osteopath who has the letters MRO after his/her name. A possible alternative would be MBNOA (see *Naturopathy*).

PARACETAMOL

A useful drug for relieving pain and lowering raised temperature. Since 1986, there has been a massive switchover to this drug from aspirin by parents, because of the announcement by the British government's Departments of Health that aspirin should no longer be given to children, in view of the risk of Reye's syndrome (see *Aspirin* and *Reye's syndrome*).

Paracetamol is about as effective as aspirin as a pain-killer, and is also useful in childhood fevers. However, it lacks aspirin's 'anti-inflammation' effect.

It doesn't cause the major side-effect of aspirin – irritation of the stomach – and it hasn't (so far, anyway) been linked in any way with Reye's syndrome. The liquid preparations are easy to give to children.

But *please* remember that paracetamol *is* a drug – even though people think of it as something very mild.

If – like most parents – you're going to keep it in your home instead of aspirin, I beg you to bear in mind that fatal overdoses of paracetamol do occur in children. The great danger is that your child may decide to help herself to some more of those nice tablets (or that nice syrup), and so kill herself!

Indeed, as the parents of Britain turn from aspirin to paracetamol, I reckon it's quite inevitable that deaths from paracetamol poisoning are going to occur. *A vital point:* if your child does go and help herself to some paracetamol, don't be misled into a false sense of security by the fact that she seems quite well afterwards. Typically, what happens is that the child *seems* well for two or three days – and then succumbs to fatal liver damage.

You have been warned: lock up your paracetamol where children cannot possibly get at it!

Having said all that, I have to admit that paracetamol in reasonable dosage is a very useful drug. Here are the correct dosages for each age group:

Under one year: 60 to 120 milligrammes every four to six hours

Aged one to five years: 120 to 250 milligrammes every four to six hours

Aged six to twelve years: 250 to 500 milligrammes every four to six hours

Finally, since so many people are badly muddled about which pain-killing preparations contain paracetamol, here's a list of some common ones. (For a list of common aspirin-containing pain-killers, see *Aspirin*.)

Some common paracetamol-containing preparations

Angier's Junior Paracetamol	*Panadol soluble tablets*
Cafadol	*Panadol tablets*
Calpol suspension	*Panasorb tablets*
Hedex	*Paracetamol elixir*
Junior Disprol	*Paracetamol tablets*
Paldesic syrup	
Panadol elixir	*Salzone syrup*

PETIT MAL

This brief mental 'absence' is seen in many children with epilepsy. See *Epilepsy*.

PHENYLKETONURIA *(PKU)*

This rare but very important inherited disorder is important because:
- if untreated, it causes mental subnormality
- it can be picked up soon after birth by a screening test on the child's blood;
- once it's been picked up, then adjustment of the child's diet will prevent the mental subnormality.

There are now many children running around happily, with completely normal intelligence – because the screening test detected their phenylketonuria.

PKU occurs in one in 20,000 babies in the UK. Although it's inherited, parents will have no idea that they are carrying the gene for phenylketonuria. It's only when two people who are both carrying this gene have a child that the disease may occur.

At birth, the youngster appears perfectly normal. But if the disease wasn't detected, then he'd fairly soon develop weight loss, vomiting, lack of appetite and irritability. Convulsions sometimes occur, eczema is common, so is hyperactivity (see *Hyperactivity*). Mental impairment eventually occurs in 98 per cent of children.

A curious marker is that many of these children are fair-haired, fair-skinned and blue-eyed – because they're short of the dark pigment melanin.

The defective gene makes the child deficient in a liver enzyme called phenylalaninase. Its job in the body is to break down a natural body chemical called phenylalanine. In children with PKU, the concentration of phenylalanine in the blood rapidly rises to dangerous levels, and causes all the symptoms mentioned – including mental defect.

Now a breakdown product of this stuff is passed out in the child's urine. A screening test, invented about thirty years ago, will detect it in the nappy. But in Britain, we now use a more accurate test (the Guthrie test) done on the child's blood when he's about six days old. This only involves a small jab in the heel, and it's vital that you should agree to your new baby having it done, even though PKU is so rare.

If PKU does turn out to be present, then the great thing is that a special diet which keeps the phenylalanine level low should give the child a normal intelligence. But it should be started before he's about two weeks old.

PIMPLES

Pimples in young children are seldom troublesome, and can usually be ignored.

However, pimples occurring as a part of nappy rash may indicate infection, and should be shown to your doctor or health visitor (see *Nappy rash*).

Pimples occurring between the thighs may be embarrassing for a child. They may be due to chafing, or to a skin fungus infection – check with your doctor.

Pimples in older children usually indicate mild or early acne (see *Acne*).

PLEURISY

Pleurisy (sometimes known as pleuritis) is an inflammation of the membrane which surrounds the lungs. It's now quite rare in the UK, but when it happens it can make the child very ill and be distressing – mainly because it tends to cause intense pain on deep breathing.

Pleurisy is usually secondary to some other chest problem, such as pneumonia (see *Pneumonia*). The child needs to be admitted to hospital, but with antibiotic and other treatment, should make a good recovery.

PNEUMONIA *(Pneumonitis)*

This means inflammation of the lung. There are lots of different kinds of pneumonia. Infants are most liable to the kind called bronchopneumonia; and older children are more likely to get lobar pneumonia. In the old days (as you'll have gathered from reading novels), all kinds of pneumonia were very likely to kill a child, but in this antibiotic age, most youngsters make a good and complete recovery.

Bronchopneumonia is a generalized lung and air-tube infection which may develop from a cold which has gone to the chest. Symptoms are breathlessness, cough and high temperature. Particularly if she's small, the baby may well need to be admitted to hospital, for oxygen tent and antibiotic therapy. Some cases are milder, and a bigger child might possibly be nursed at home.

Lobar pneumonia is an infection which affects one lobe (or piece) of the lung. The old term 'double pneumonia' means that two lobes are affected.

Symptoms include barking cough, fever, shivering, blueness of the skin, rusty-brown sputum and breathlessness. Your doctor will probably want an x-ray to confirm the diagnosis. Modern antibiotics (such as penicillin) usually produce a very fast recovery.

POISONING

See *First Aid*.

POLIO

Polio, poliomyelitis or infantile paralysis is a very serious virus infection which until about 1960 used to kill or paralyse many children.

The wonderfully effective polio vaccine has almost put an end to these tragedies. Almost – but not quite. A few deaths and cases of paralysis do still occur, mainly because a lot of parents don't have the sense to get their kids immunized!

The little polio virus passed from person to person with horrifying ease. It was thought that the germ was passed out in an infected child's bowel motions and that poor toilet hygiene (i.e. failing to wash the hands after passing a motion) helped to pass it on. However, even today we're not certain of how it is spread.

But in the 1950s there were a series of medical developments in the USA. Scientists there discovered how to grow polio virus in the laboratory. Then the great Dr Salk used this knowledge to develop an injectable vaccine against polio – which meant that literally millions of children's lives would be saved.

Later, another American researcher – Dr Albert Sabin – invented a vaccine which could be taken by mouth, so there is now no need even to undergo a jab. Three drops on a sugar lump give almost complete protection.

So polio, only 30 years ago the cause of so much death and misery, has now been virtually banished from most Western countries. But that doesn't mean that you needn't bother to get your youngsters immunized – polio could come back at any time if parents don't take the trouble to get their babies protected. Alarming little outbreaks can occur when mums and dads don't bother to get their kids done any more. For the best times for giving the drops, consult the schedule in *Immunization*.

It is important to remember that there is still a tremendous amount of polio about in many tropical and sub-tropical countries – and this includes popular holiday areas like North Africa, Mexico and parts of the West Indies.

So if you're off to, say, Tunisia or

Barbados, you should make sure that not just the children but all the adults in the party have up-to-date immunization if they don't want to end up paralysed – or dead. Polio is the travel immunization that most often seems to get forgotten, and in several summers of research on behalf of both BBC-TV and *General Practitioner*, I've found that many travel firms and airlines never even think of mentioning it.

If you're on holiday in a hot country or in Scandinavia (where there's been some polio in recent years) and your youngster develops a temperature, an off-colour feeling and a headache, with perhaps some vomiting, then put him to bed and call a doctor. Rest is believed to be the best therapy for polio, but sadly there's little else that can be done to fight the established infection. Antibiotics don't work at all, because this is a virus.

The symptoms I've described, of course, are typical of countless other minor childhood illnesses. However, the thing to bear in mind is this: if you've had your child immunized against the disease by taking the drops, then it's most unlikely that wherever you go in the world you'll have to worry about polio.

By the way: is *your* polio protection up-to-date? Adults can easily catch it, specially if they travel abroad. And just before this book went to press, it was reported that two fathers had been paralysed by the disease simply because their children had been given the drops – and the virus from the drops had spread to the fathers.

Because of the slight risk of such tragedies, the latest official advice is that if an unvaccinated father or mother wants his or her child to have polio drops, then the parent should have the drops too.

PSORIASIS

Psoriasis is one of the most common of all skin disorders, with well over a million sufferers in the UK. However, it's not often seen in young children, and the incidence doesn't start to rise rapidly until later childhood.

There are two things you need to know about psoriasis:

- it's *not* infectious, and has nothing to do with dirt or lack of cleanliness
- the actual cause isn't known.

Youngsters with psoriasis can have a very difficult time because classmates, and sometimes even teachers, think that they're infectious or 'dirty'.

But the plaque-like crusty eruptions of psoriasis aren't even remotely infectious. I've been prodding the skins of people with psoriasis for twenty-five years, and so far haven't caught anything!

Treatment includes peeling agents such as dithranol paste or ointment (though this has to be used with extreme caution in childhood), tar and salicylic acid applications, tar baths and steroid ointments or creams (again, these must be used with caution in childhood).

'PUVA therapy' – which involves exposure to ultra-violet light – seems to have helped many patients, but discuss possible long-term side-effects with your child's dermatologist. Finally, you should most definitely join:

The Psoriasis Association
7 Milton Street
Northampton
NN2 7JG

PYLORIC STENOSIS

This is a narrowing of the tube which carries food out of the baby's stomach (see picture below).

This moderately common disorder of young babies (age one to twelve weeks) affects more boys than girls.

What happens is that the muscle round the tube leading out of the stomach becomes swollen, and the swelling 'comes up' whenever the child has a feed. We don't know why this swelling should occur, but the great thing is that it's easily cured these days.

The main symptom is forceful vomiting – what is called projectile vomiting. This means that your baby is so violently sick that he may quite literally be able to hit the wall on the other side of the room!

Not only is this extremely distressing for the baby (and the mother), but it's very dangerous as well. For within a few days, the baby is usually vomiting after every feed, with the result that he is getting no fluid and no nutrition whatsoever.

Without rapid treatment, he would die. In fact, many babies do become seriously dehydrated (i.e. short of fluid) before anybody realizes what's happened.

The diagnosis of pyloric stenosis can be quite difficult. But the doctor will be very suspicious that this condition is present if a baby who has previously been well suddenly develops projectile vomiting at some age between about one and twelve weeks.

If the doctor examines the baby's tummy while he's feeding she will probably be able to feel the hard swelling

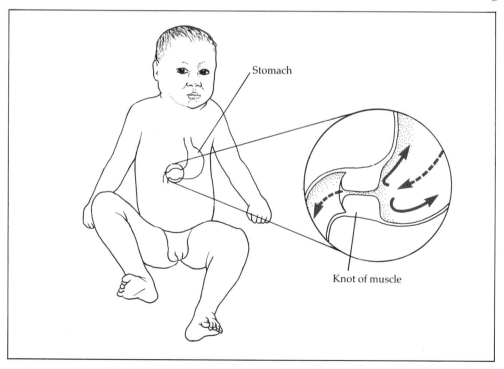

Stomach

Knot of muscle

developing at the lower end of the stomach. She may also be able to see telltale powerful waves of contraction sweeping across the baby's stomach as it tries in vain to empty itself through the blocked exit.

Your baby may have a special barium meal x-ray to help confirm the diagnosis.

The outlook for these seriously ill babies was revolutionized in 1913 when a German surgeon called Conrad Ramstedt invented the operation which is still in use today. It just involves opening the child's abdomen and making a small cut in the tight knot of muscle at the exit of the stomach. Doing this is sufficient to allow the food to pass out of the stomach in the normal way – and so the operation usually produces a complete cure.

Non-surgical treatment (i.e. with drugs) is sometimes tried – particularly in the early stages, when it may not be quite clear whether the child really has got pyloric stenosis or not. The drugs which are given are atropine derivatives, such as Eumydrine. They are antispasmodics, intended to combat the spasm of the muscle at the pylorus.

In addition, the baby may have to have a drip in order to restore all the fluid he has lost.

After recovering from the operation, the baby should go on to lead a normal healthy life. In fact, when one does routine examinations of healthy teenagers and adults, it's quite common to see on their tummies the small discreet scar of a successful Ramstedt's operation which saved their lives many years before.

QUINSY

This is a painful and distressing abscess which comes up next to the child's tonsil, making swallowing very difficult. It may occur after tonsillitis (see *Tonsillitis*) or a tooth extraction.

Fast treatment with antibiotics is effective, but it may be necessary for a surgeon to cut open the quinsy (this is normally done under anaesthetic), in order to release the pus inside.

RASHES

These are, of course, among the most common symptoms seen in children. Their diagnosis frequently baffles or confuses trained doctors – so there's no way I can make you an expert in rashes through the medium of this book!

So, when do you have to take a rash seriously and ring your doctor?

Fortunately, most childhood rashes *aren't* serious, and are due to trivial causes like chafing, insect bites or some minor allergy.

But always ring your doctor if your child has a rash that is: accompanied by a high temperature (over 37·8°C or 100°F); or accompanied by a severe headache or mental confusion.

Also, you should of course ring your doctor if your child has a rash after being in contact with an infectious disease of childhood, such as measles or German measles.

Note that I say '*ring* your doctor'. I continue to be amazed at the number of parents who think that it's OK to take a child who may have (say) German measles down to their GP's surgery –

where he may sit down alongside an expectant mum.

The rashes of the common infectious childhood diseases are described – with pictures – under *Chickenpox; German measles; Fifth Disease; Measles* and *Roseola*. See also *Scarlet Fever*.

Finally, what do you do about rashes which aren't associated with any of the warning signals which I've mentioned above?

As these are likely to be due to non-serious causes, many will go away within a few hours on their own account. But if a rash persists for a day or so (and especially if it's itchy or causing the child distress), then it's perfectly reasonable to make an appointment for the child to see your GP.

For other possible causes of such persistent rashes see *Allergies; Eczema; Urticaria; Ringworm* or other fungus infection; rarely scabies; cat, flea or other insect bites (far more common than people think!).

REYE'S SYNDROME

Reye's syndrome (it rhymes with 'eyes') has started hitting the headlines recently. Shortly before this book was published, there was a sensation in Britain when Government health advisers announced that because of a suggested link between aspirin products and Reye's syndrome, children under the age of twelve should no longer be given aspirin. Naturally, this alarmed many parents.

What *is* Reye's syndrome? It's a very serious disease of the brain and liver. It attacks children who are recovering from some relatively minor illness –

especially 'flu or chickenpox, but it can occur with a lot of other childhood infections too.

And the extraordinary thing is that it seems quite likely that the syndrome is in some way 'triggered off' by aspirin.

Admittedly, the link with aspirin is still not entirely *proved*. But the suspicion is now so very great that in the UK, it is no longer possible to buy 'junior aspirin' – and warnings are being put on ordinary aspirin preparations, telling parents not to give them to children under twelve.

There's one exception to this startling new ruling: a doctor may still prescribe aspirin in conditions such as childhood arthritis, in which she or he feels that the benefits of giving it outweigh the risk of Reye's syndrome.

How great *are* those risks? In Britain the best estimates at the moment are that Reye's affects about six children out of every million per year. (The rate in America appears to be rather higher.)

That may not sound much. But in practice it means that every year about 60 British children are being diagnosed as having Reye's syndrome. And I have to be quite blunt and say that the death rate in Reye's syndrome is very high – around about 50 per cent at the moment. Only rapid hospitalization (preferably into an intensive care unit with life support facilities) is likely to give a reasonable chance of saving the child's life.

Clearly then, every parent ought to know the symptoms of Reye's.

- In most cases, just as a child starts getting better after some relatively minor infection, she suddenly starts *vomiting* – and the vomiting is severe and repeated.
- Other possible symptoms are: de-

liriousness, fits, lethargy, staring into space, spasms of the arms or legs, screaming attacks and unconsciousness.

Obviously, if your child develops *any* of these symptoms while making a recovery from an ordinary childhood infection such as chickenpox or influenza, you *must* get on the phone to your doctor immediately – even if the youngster has been given no aspirin at all. Don't hesitate to say that you are worried about the possibility of Reye's.

I wish I could explain to you *why* all the above symptoms occur. But all we can say at the moment is that they appear to be caused by a malfunction of the brain and the liver. And the very strong suspicion is that this malfunction is somehow provoked by giving the child aspirin.

The aspirin link is very difficult to prove with certainty – simply because most children who are ill with chickenpox, 'flu and other childhood fevers have tended to be given aspirin by parents or doctors.

However, the preliminary results of both American and British studies do strongly suggest a link. The British authorities seem to have been prompted to ban children's aspirin when they learned that in the USA, the simple process of putting a 'Parents' Health Warning' on aspirin packs had apparently reduced the number of cases of Reye's syndrome.

A further factor in Britain has been the highly effective publicity campaign against aspirin waged by the National Reye's Syndrome Foundation, led by Mrs Audrey Harrington – a mother who tragically lost her own daughter through Reye's syndrome.

At the time this book goes to press, I personally feel that the case against aspirin is not totally proven. But the level of governmental and parental concern is such that I would not give a child under the age of about 14 any aspirin-containing preparation unless there were some very strong reason for it.

So what do you turn to instead of aspirin?

First, bear in mind that the conditions for which you *might* have given aspirin (primarily pain and/or raised temperature) do often respond at least moderately well to a kiss and a cuddle – which have *no* side-effects at all!

To bring down a raised temperature, you should use the commonsense methods of cooling described elsewhere in this book (see *Feverish convulsions*).

Secondly, we're now seeing a massive switch-over by parents from aspirin to paracetamol. But do please remember that it IS a drug, too, and that fatal poisoning from it does occur. So if you use it on your child, lock it away afterwards so that she can't help herself to it.

Many parents are muddled about just which preparations contain aspirin, and which contain paracetamol. For a guide to the common products containing these drugs, see *Aspirin* and *Paracetamol*.

RHESUS FACTOR

Rhesus factor used to be a big problem for many babies only a generation or so ago. Fortunately, the problem is now pretty well cracked, thanks to a remarkable injection which is given just after childbirth to mothers who are 'rhesus negative'.

To sum up a very complicated subject, if you checked the blood groups of

100 British people, you'd find that about 85 of them were 'rhesus positive', and about 15 'rhesus negative'.

If a rhesus negative woman becomes pregnant by a rhesus positive man, there's a risk that she may form antibodies against rhesus positive blood, just after the baby is delivered.

This is not significant unless she becomes pregnant *again* with a rhesus positive baby. If that happens, then her antibodies may attack this baby's blood, causing anaemia (weakness of the blood) and jaundice (see *Jaundice*).

Unfortunately, this jaundice may be so bad that it damages the child's brain – though it's possible to keep the level of jaundice down by the rather difficult process of giving the baby repeated changes of blood.

It's now possible to give newly-delivered rhesus negative mothers an injection which stops them from developing antibodies in the first place. Ideally, this jab should also be given immediately after an abortion or a miscarriage, in order to safeguard future babies.

RHEUMATIC FEVER

This once common childhood condition is now – mercifully – very rare in Britain. It used to cause severe heart valve damage in many children. Rheumatic fever seems to be an odd reaction to a throat infection caused by a very common germ, the streptococcus.

Seven to twenty-one days after a throat infection the child develops quite severe pain and swelling in one or more of the large joints (e.g. knee, elbow, ankle). The pain tends to flit around from joint to joint.

The joint pain always goes away eventually, but the risk of heart valve damage is great. This damage may lead to breathlessness, weakness and severe disability. (However, these days cardiac surgery can be carried out to cure or improve the trouble.)

Treatment of rheumatic fever is with bed-rest, aspirin and sometimes steroid (cortisone-like) drugs.

RHEUMATOID ARTHRITIS

Unfortunately (and surprisingly) rheumatoid arthritis does sometimes occur in children. So too does the similar form of arthritis called Still's disease. (See *Still's Disease*. Slightly confusingly, some doctors use the expression 'Still's disease' to mean rheumatoid arthritis.)

Girls are affected three times as often as boys. Symptoms include persistent and very distressing pains in the joints, plus swelling and stiffness, especially in the hands.

Treatment is with aspirin and/or other anti-inflammatory drugs plus physiotherapy. Joint replacement is sometimes possible. A powerful drug called penicillamine is often used these days, though very recent research has cast doubt on its effectiveness. Acupuncture will not cure the condition, but can often relieve pain.

RICKETS

This is a vitamin deficiency disease caused by lack of sunlight (which helps make vitamin D in children's skin). It is now extremely rare in the UK, except among Asian children living in sun-deficient cities like Glasgow.

The symptoms are bone and tooth deformities – including those bent legs still seen in a few older people who were children in smoggy cities more than sixty years ago.

If you let her go out in the open air and get daylight on her skin, your child is most unlikely to get rickets. But if you are an Asian parent who believes in strict covering of the skin, your child could run into problems. Ask your child health clinic's advice about vitamin D supplements – and also about using vitamin D-fortified chappati flour.

RINGWORM

This is a very common infection, especially in country districts, where the child may easily catch it through contact with animals (especially cattle).

It's a fungus infection of the skin (no connection with worms!), and it produces an itchy, red crusty area on the child's skin. Very often, the affected area has the curved edge that gives ringworm its name. On the scalp, ringworm will often cause a patch of hair loss (see picture above).

Most children can be successfully treated with an anti-fungus cream or ointment prescribed by your doctor. But please bear in mind that the ringworm will probably come back if the cream isn't used regularly – and until about two weeks after all visible trace of ringworm has gone.

Very occasionally, a child whose ringworm doesn't respond to local applications may need a powerful oral drug called griseofulvin.

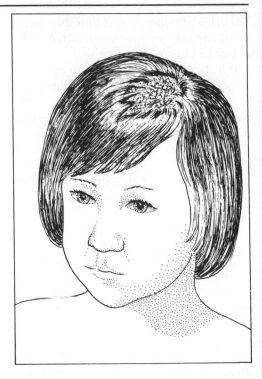

ROSEOLA *(Roseola Infantum)*

Although the name isn't well known to most parents, this is actually one of the four common feverish rashes of childhood – along with measles, German measles and chickenpox. Its alternative name is Exanthem subitum.

There's a very good chance that your baby may get it, some time between the ages of six months and two years.

Doctors haven't yet been able to isolate the germ of roseola, but from the way that children react when they've got it, it seems almost certain that the cause of the symptom is a viral agent – probably acquired when the baby breathes in air-borne droplets which have been breathed out by someone carrying the virus.

Now to symptoms. As I've indicated

above, the most dramatic symptom of roseola infantum is the rash which it produces. But that isn't the first symptom.

In fact, the first sign that something is wrong comes when your baby suddenly develops quite a high temperature – often in the region of 38·9°C (102°F).

This fever comes on about ten days after your baby has been exposed to the virus – or so doctors believe. However, in practice you're never likely to find out just who it was who gave your baby the virus. (If it was an adult, he or she probably seemed perfectly well.)

After about four days of raised temperature – and probably just about the time when you're beginning to get rather worried about *why* your child is so hot – then quite suddenly, his temperature falls to normal. And just when you think that the illness is all over, the baby surprises you by coming out in a mysterious rash! That's the characteristic feature of roseola: it can be very puzzling indeed if you don't know what's wrong!

The rash is a reddish, speckly one (see picture) which develops quite rapidly all over the body. It's particularly marked behind the ears. There are no lumps, and no fluid-filled blobs of the kind you get with chickenpox.

Don't panic if you see such a rash. You should let your GP know some time within the next twelve hours or so, but there's no need to call him out in the small hours of the morning to look at it.

Happily, your baby remains perfectly well and cheerful during the rash stage of the infection – because he's feeling a good deal better than he was during the high temperature stage.

Within about a day of appearing, the rash disappears. From that point on, the

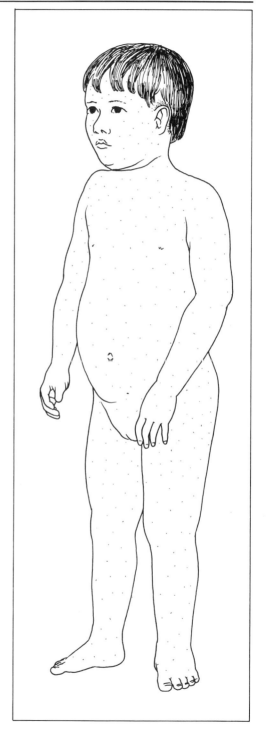

infection is over, and you can forget all about it.

A little paracetamol will help bring the temperature down, but there is no point in giving antibiotics. Give him plenty of cool drinks – this is a good practice with any child who has a sky-high temperature.

Once the temperature has fallen and the baby is in the rash stage of roseola, no further treatment is usually necessary. For by then, he's usually on the road to recovery.

RUBELLA

See *German measles*.

RUPTURE

See *Hernia*.

ST VITUS' DANCE *(Sydenham's chorea)*

This disorder in which a child mysteriously becomes restless and fidgety and cannot keep her arms or legs still, is now quite rare.

It is thought to be due to an odd reaction to an infection, which somehow affects the brain centres which are concerned with muscle control and movement. Some parents mistakenly punish the child for being fidgety – *don't*: she can't help it.

The main treatment is just rest in bed, and most children make a complete recovery in a few weeks or months.

SCALDS

See *Burns and scalds* under *First Aid*.

SCARS

Scars following injury, burns or surgery can be very distressing for a child, and indeed for her parents.

Plastic surgery can often help in removing such scars, but it can't achieve miracles, and there are many cases where plastic surgery simply won't help.

You have to remember that the results of plastic surgery aren't always perfect. Quite a number of children have the kind of skins that respond to surgical incisions by forming a mass of raised, smooth tissue called a keloid. This is a particular problem among black children, and it may sometimes make the results of plastic surgery look rather disappointing.

In fact, many doctors prefer to treat scars by suggesting some sort of cosmetic disguise. It may be difficult to accept that all that can be done for your child's scarring is the use of cosmetics. But in fact, once you've been taught their careful and skilled use you may be delighted by their results.

Of course, you shouldn't just buy any old make-up and try and disguise your child's scars with it. Contact one of the manufacturers listed in the table under *Birthmarks*.

SCARLET FEVER *(Scarlatina)*

Scarlet fever used to be a very serious disease, which killed many children each year.

Nowadays, things have changed. Although many parents may be worried at hearing the phrase 'scarlet fever', it is *not* a very serious disease in Britain any more. We don't know why this is, but it seems to have changed its nature. Quite often, it consists only of a sore throat, and a bit of a pink blotchiness.

But serious complications can occasionally occur, so its best to be aware of them if your doctor diagnoses scarlet fever in your toddler or schoolchild.

Scarlet fever is caused by a common germ called the streptococcus. This is very often present in people's throats, and we've all had it at some time or other. It usually causes hoarseness, and it can be responsible for ear ache.

However, in some children (who seem to be especially susceptible to the germ) it produces scarlet fever instead. This is characterized by a sore throat or a bout of tonsillitis – accompanied by a red rash which covers the child's face and her whole body (see picture). This odd reaction seems to be due to a chemical which is produced by the germ when it invades the child's body.

The incubation period of scarlet fever is about two to six days. Your child will probably have picked it up from a symptomless carrier, rather than from someone who clearly has scarlet fever.

To begin with, the youngster suddenly becomes ill, with a rise in temperature to about 39·4°C (103°F), a general feeling of being off-colour, a sore throat and very frequently vomiting and loss of appetite.

A couple of days later she'll come out in the characteristic red rash. In years gone by this really used to be very bright scarlet, but nowadays it may be little more than a pinkish discolouration of the skin, which disappears within about

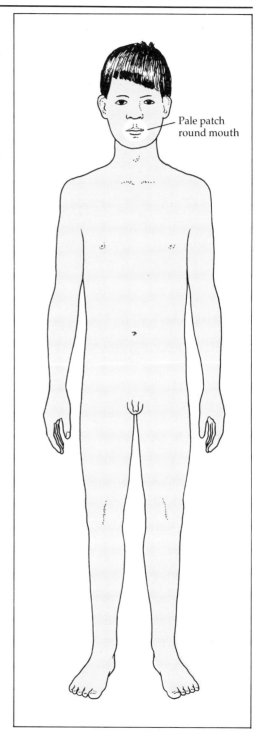

Pale patch round mouth

a week. You may also notice that her tongue looks like an unripe strawberry – whitish, with little red spots in the early stages.

If you think your child has scarlet fever, keep her in bed and contact your doctor. He will probably treat her with penicillin, and advise keeping her at home for a week or ten days.

Both you and your doctor should be on the look-out for the occasional complications of scarlet fever. These are:

- Kidney inflammation (see *Nephritis*) – a problem which sometimes occurs about the third week after the start of the rash. Some doctors feel that because of the small risk of kidney trouble, any child who has had scarlet fever should have a urine specimen examined about three weeks after the onset of the infection, just in case.
- Rheumatic fever (see *Rheumatic fever*). This is very rare these days, but if your youngster gets severe pain in her joints a few weeks after the onset of scarlet fever, then you'd better put her to bed and contact your doctor.
- Ear ache. This is an occasional complication, due to the fact that the streptococcus does like finding its way from the throat up into the ear and causing trouble. The treatment is as for ordinary ear ache (see *Ear ache*).

SCHOOL PHOBIA *(and playschool phobia)*

Yes, this *is* an illness! Of course, a lot of children who've got nothing at all wrong with them do try to get out of going to school (or, indeed, playschool)

for no very good reason. With them, you just have to be very firm!

But there may be an important reason why a child tries to refuse to go to school or playschool. The three most common are probably bullying, fear or dislike of a particular teacher or distress about some unhappy situation at home.

If you suspect one or other of the first two reasons, go and see the head teacher and try to sort the problem out with her.

The third reason is pretty frequent too. If your child keeps bunking off school at a time when you and your spouse are at daggers drawn, or when one of you has just walked out on the other, then the reason for the youngster's behaviour is fairly obvious.

Sometimes, the child's aversion to school is so great that he really cannot overcome it without professional help. In these cases, there's no point in asking your GP for tranquillizers (either for the child or for you!). It's far better to ask the school to arrange for the youngster to see an educational psychologist – whose job it is to try to unravel behaviour difficulties such as this.

SCURVY

This illness is caused by deficiency of vitamin C – the vitamin found in fruit and green vegetables and also potatoes.

Scurvy used to be quite common in British babies a generation or so ago, but is now very rare, mainly due to better nutrition and in particular the widespread supplementary use (since World War II) of orange juice for young babies.

Breast milk normally contains enough vitamin C to prevent scurvy, but bottle-fed babies should have 50 ml of fresh orange or tomato juice a day (*not* boiled – this destroys the vitamin).

Warning. Some paediatricians claim that if a mother takes vitamin C during pregnancy to ward off colds, this may make the baby accustomed to too high a level of it – with the result that he'll develop scurvy some months after birth.

Scurvy usually arises between the age of six months and two and a half years. It's characterized by irritability, bone pain, bleeding into the gums and the curious 'frog positions' which the child probably assumes in order to relieve the pain in his leg bones.

Treatment is with large doses of vitamin C – which should be curative if given early enough.

SEA SICKNESS

See *Travel sickness*.

SICKLE CELL ANAEMIA

This uncommon and very trying form of anaemia (weakness of the blood) is seen only in children of West Indian or African stock.

The disease is due to a faulty gene, carried by about 10 per cent of British West Indians and by many Africans. However, carrying this faulty gene causes virtually no problems at all, and most carriers never even know that they have it. But if two carriers have a child, there's a one in four chance that she'll have sickle cell anaemia. Simple calculation shows that this is fortunately a rare

occurrence, but it's a tragedy for a child when it occurs.

Why? Because the features of sickle cell anaemia are severe growth stunting, weakness, tiredness, debility, jaundice and bouts of intense pains in the limbs. (Most books say that the disease may easily be mistaken for appendicitis, but in fact this is rare.)

At present there is no cure. It's best to get the child treated by a specialist unit which knows how to handle the severe, painful crises of sickle cell anaemia with drip treatment.

A new test may eventually make it routine for at-risk mothers to find out very early in pregnancy whether the baby would have sickle cell anaemia.

SINUSITIS

This is rare in young children, partly because the sinuses (which are air pockets inside the bones of the skull) aren't fully developed in early life. You can see where the sinuses are from the picture overleaf: there are four sets behind the face.

But sinusitis is common in schoolchildren, and can cause a lot of misery. Symptoms include fever, headache, pain behind the eyes or in the cheeks, a very unpleasant blocked-up feeling and difficulty in breathing through the nose.

Infection spreads from the child's nose into her sinuses (especially after a bad cold). The sinuses have very narrow openings, so once an infection has established itself, a lot of pressure may build up – particularly if pus is being formed.

If your doctor diagnoses sinusitis, she'll usually give your child an antibi-

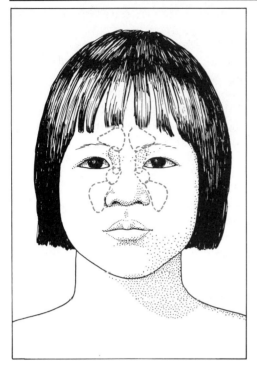

otic, plus a short course of decongestant nose-drops, in order to try and clear the sinuses. Decongestant tablets are also used.

In some children, sinusitis just keeps going on and on, so that the youngster's life becomes a misery. In this case, ask your doctor to send her to an ear, nose and throat specialist, who'll advise you whether an operation to improve the drainage of the sinuses is necessary.

SNAKE BITES

In mainland Britain, there's only one poisonous snake (the adder or viper) and bites from it are very rare. There are no snakes in Ireland.

However, if you take your children on holiday to some areas of Europe (not-ably the mountainous regions of Italy and south west France), there are enough vipers around to make summer hill-walking just a little risky! In these areas, many *gîtes* and holiday farm-houses keep a supply of anti-snake bite serum in the fridge.

If your child is bitten by a snake:
1 Don't panic – death is very rare;
2 Calm him down;
3 Don't go in for cowboy-type lunacies like sticking knives into the wound or trying to suck the venom out;
4 Get the child to medical help as fast as possible, *keeping the bitten part elevated*;
5 Don't use tourniquets, as they can cause *gangrene* (except in expert hands);
6 If you have access to anti-viper serum, make sure you give the correct dose for a child *and no more*. In danger areas of Europe, pharmacists invariably stock the serum and should know the correct dose.

SNORING

Don't make a big deal of it if your child snores – at least 50 per cent of young-sters do. While it matters if a husband or wife snores loudly (for obvious reasons), it really doesn't matter a hoot if a child snores.

However, very loud and persistent snoring, associated with difficulty in getting the breath, may indicate either adenoid trouble (see *Adenoids*) or catarrh (see *Catarrh*) or both. Your GP may possibly want to refer the child to an ear, nose and throat specialist.

Hypnotism is occasionally used to treat snoring too.

SORE THROAT

A sore throat is, of course, one of the most common of all symptoms, both in adults and in children. It's normally caused by infection – but irritation (e.g. by cigarette smoke) may play a part.

Oddly enough though, most young children don't actually complain of soreness in the throat. They usually just feel unwell, and may cough, or be sick. In fact, in small children throat infection is really exactly the same thing as tonsillitis (see *Tonsillitis*).

In older children, a sore throat is exactly the same as an adult's sore throat. One very important point which you should understand as a parent is this. At least half of all childhood sore throats are caused by a virus: this means, that no antibiotic in the world will have any effect on them. (Penicillin and other antibiotics only work on bacteria – not viruses.)

So if your child gets a sore throat, keep her at home, and give her lots of fluid and a little paracetamol.

The proprietary throat lozenges, sweets and sprays, which you can buy cheaply from a chemist are soothing, though there's some doubt about whether they really do much good.

If a child really feels terrible with a sore throat – or if it goes on for some days – then that's a different matter. There is a possibility that the infection may be bacterial, rather than viral, and in that case the doctor will prescribe antibiotics, especially if she feels that the infection is spreading.

I have to add that many doctors prescribe antibiotics – rather defensively! – for *all* sore throats, because of the difficulty of deciding whether the infection

is bacterial or viral. And a few are daft enough to make a habit of leaving out antibiotic prescriptions to be collected – without even seeing the child, or her throat. Naturally, this can lead to such unfortunate occurrences as a failure to diagnose more serious illnesses.

Clinical ecologists do quite rightly point out that dust and smoke can irritate the human throat. Parents' cigarette smoke is almost certainly a major factor in aggravating sore throats in children.

SPASTIC DISORDERS *(Cerebral palsy)*

It's a tragedy that so many children are born spastic – i.e. suffering from cerebral palsy.

Let's just explain those two terms first. The word spastic means 'associated with spasm of the muscles'. Many parents dislike this word – partly because people tend to use it thoughtlessly as a term of abuse. (Do try and prevent your youngsters from saying things like 'You silly spastic', which can cause great distress.) So the word will probably soon be dropped in favour of 'cerebral palsy'. Palsy means paralysis, and cerebral means to do with the brain.

Cerebral palsy is caused by brain injury – usually occurring either in the mother's womb, or at childbirth.

In many cases, it's nobody's *fault* that this brain injury has occurred. But there are some instances where it's due to mismanagement of labour – and here the parents would have a claim against the Health Authority and the medical staff involved.

The symptoms of cerebral palsy vary depending on which part of the brain has been affected. In all cases, movement of the child's limbs and/or face is affected in some way.

There may also be involuntary movements or co-ordination problems, particularly with speech. In some cerebral palsy children, there may be additional difficulties with epilepsy (see *Epilepsy*) or blindness or deafness. Also, some children are mentally handicapped.

But it's vital to understand that many children with cerebral palsy have perfectly normal intelligence. Sadly, this is often very difficult for other people to grasp. Until they realize the truth, some adults and children treat cerebral palsy youngsters as if they were idiots! In fact, to give just one example, there are now quite a lot of excellent and entertaining books (many of them much better than this one, I dare say) which have been written by people with cerebral palsy.

I'm afraid drugs cannot cure cerebral palsy, and play little or no part in treatment. What's needed is very intensive education of the child's brain to help her cope with the skills of life – and particularly of communication with other people.

Physiotherapy, occupational therapy, speech therapy and specialized teaching all play a part. Orthopaedic surgery may help a contracted limb. Obviously, the establishment in recent years of some excellent schools for the handicapped and the invention of mechanical aids has helped a lot of cerebral palsy children to develop their skills.

But most of the burden still falls on the parents. Their efforts in helping the child 'stretch' herself and in providing as happy and stable a home life as possible are of enormous importance to her future development.

But the establishment of organizations like Riding For The Disabled and the Cerebral Palsy Association provide a great back-up. In addition, parents will probably want to get in touch with their local branch of the Spastics Society. Write to them at:

12 Park Crescent
London W1N 4EQ

Alternative therapy

Both **osteopaths** and **chiropractors** feel that they can sometimes help 'ease' a contracted limb by massage.

In America, Britain and Hungary, organizations aiming to 'increase human potential' have treated many cerebral palsy children with intensive programmes of exercises, task-solving, and all sorts of stimuli.

Although their approach to publicity has upset some doctors, and although the treatment can be expensive, it seems to me that this sort of 'intensive care' may help the child to progress and develop.

SPOTS

See *Rashes*; also *Acne*.

SPRAINS

These are 'twists' of a joint, without anything being actually broken. Most childhood sprains respond well to: rest; gentle compression with a bandage; cool applications – especially ice (or a packet of frozen peas!) wrapped in a towel.

But if there's a lot of pain – or if it's persistent – then bear in mind that this could indicate a fracture (i.e. a break). In these circumstances, take the child to a doctor or an accident and emergency department to see if an x-ray is needed.

SQUINT

A squint must never be ignored.

So pay no attention to anybody (even if – as happens on rare occasions – it's a doctor or nurse) who says 'Oh, don't worry – she'll grow out of it.' Beware also of people who say 'Oh, it's just a lazy eye.' There is no such thing as a lazy eye.

Admittedly, some children who appear to squint are not actually doing so. The appearance may be caused by a brief inturning of the eye, or by an unusual configuration of the bridge of the nose.

But a genuine and persistent squint must be checked by an eye surgeon. This is because an untreated squint can rapidly lead to permanent loss of vision in one eye.

The surgeon will decide whether 'patching' the eye is sufficient, or whether an operation is necessary. He or she will also arrange for an optometrist to give the child special eye exercises in due course.

STAMMERING

See *Stuttering*.

STILL'S DISEASE

This is a childhood form of arthritis – i.e. joint disease. Very confusingly, some doctors use the term Still's disease to mean the juvenile form of rheumatoid arthritis (see *Rheumatoid arthritis*).

Others use the expression to mean a slightly different condition. Features include joint pain (sometimes severe), with episodes of fever and rashes. Eye trouble sometimes occurs too.

Treatment is with anti-inflammatory drugs, plus physiotherapy, hydrotherapy and (where necessary) bed-rest and temporary splinting of joints.

Cortisone-like drugs and ACTH (pituitary hormone) injections are frequently used, but can have major side-effects.

Although this is a very trying condition (for both child and parents) the outlook is much better than it used to be.

STINGS

See *First Aid*.

STOMACH ACHE

See *Abdominal pain*.

STRESS IN CHILDHOOD

Yes, there is such a thing as stress in childhood – something that a lot of adults seem to find very hard to understand. Whenever I discuss it on the radio, the presenter nearly always seems to say, 'But surely, doctor – you're not saying that children can get tummy ache/headache/whatever because of stress, are you?'

Well, that's exactly what I *am* saying. And I think every GP in the country will back me up in saying that many of the youngsters who come into the surgery complaining of physical symptoms are really suffering from some form of stress – or perhaps it'd be more reasonable to call it *dis*tress.

The symptoms which kids produce as a reaction to emotional distress seem to be usually (though not invariably) perfectly genuine to them. They're not usually putting it on, and they don't feel very well. Common symptoms are:

- tummy ache
- headache
- feeling sick
- feeling faint
- having to rush to the loo
- constipation
- burping
- tics
- nightmares.

Some children also develop irrational fears, compulsion to keep counting and checking things, or a violent aversion to going to school.

So what are the stresses which can provoke these symptoms in children. Again and again, they fall into one of two categories:

Trouble at school may involve being bullied, or being frightened of a particular teacher, or being irrationally upset about not being able to keep up with work.

Trouble at home usually seems to be related to divorce or to other marriage difficulties between the parents – but these days we're becoming increasingly aware that some children are (alas) under a lot of stress because of brutality or even sexual abuse.

A child's stress problems are virtually *never* solved by putting him or her on tranquillizers! In fact, many of these problems are eased by a sensible chat with your family doctor, or (where school seems to be the source of the problem) by a talk with the head teacher or the school's attached educational psychologist.

Difficulties at home may be much harder to resolve. Sometimes a marriage guidance counsellor can help, but if the child is reacting very badly to a fraught home situation, then your GP may suggest the type of psychotherapy called family therapy.

Of course, if you suspect that a child's stress is due to some form of physical or sexual abuse, you should of course contact the NSPCC and your local Social Services – and possibly the police.

(See also *Hysteria*; *Tics*; *Abdominal pain*)

Alternative therapy

Both **homoeopathy** and **herbalism** claim to offer remedies for stress – and these are at least likely to be much preferable to tranquillizers. But in general, the basic treatment of a child's distress is to try and remove the cause of it.

STYES

These are infections of the hair follicles from which the eyelashes grow. They're caused by the same germs which are responsible for boils.

If your child develops a stye, just bathe her eye with cotton wool dipped in warm water. Dispose of the cotton wool immediately – because it'll now have the stye's germs on it.

Once a head forms on the stye, you can release the pus (and so take away the pain) by plucking out the eyelash with a pair of tweezers. (Wash your hands – and the tweezers – very carefully afterwards.)

But if you don't want to go in for plucking out eyelashes, just carry on with the hot bathing: the stye will go within a couple of days.

There's not a lot of point in taking a child to the doctor because she has a stye. This is because neither antibiotics nor anything else can penetrate the interior of the stye. However, if your child gets recurrent styes, your doctor will almost certainly prescribe an antibiotic ointment – to prevent the stye germs from spreading to other follicles.

STUTTERING

Stuttering (which is the same thing as stammering) is very common. Nearly all of us have stuttered at some time or other when we've been nervous – and it is, in fact, nerves which play the main part in causing stuttering.

However, vast numbers of children aged between two and six do stutter a bit, simply because it's so difficult for an inexperienced young mouth to pour out all those complicated new words! Don't draw attention to your child if she does this: it's far better just to ignore it.

But if a child is clearly developing a bad stutter, then it's best to call in professional help as soon as possible. This means getting her to a speech therapist.

She will use various techniques (including the employment of earphones and metronomes) to try and restore the rhythm of the youngster's speech to normal.

The fact that this treatment usually works well is borne out by the case of the late King George VI (the Queen's father) who was terribly badly affected by a stutter when young. He was helped by a speech therapist to overcome the problem, and later made some gallant and moving speeches, which inspired many people during World War II.

In really bad cases, it may be worth considering buying a device called 'the Edinburgh masker' – which prevents the child from the stress of repeatedly hearing her own reiterated syllables, and so may help her regain normal speech. But take your speech therapist's advice first. Also, take her advice before paying out money for commercial anti-stammering courses.

SUNBURN AND SUNSTROKE

Many parents of young children don't realize that the sun (including even the weak British sun) can do a great deal of harm.

Long ago, I used to practise in a seaside town – and every week we had to deal with a fresh crop of young children who were either in severe pain from sunburn or feeling rotten from mild sunstroke.

Sunburn The best thing to do about sunburn is to prevent it, especially if your child is fair-skinned. Don't let him go out without a hat and a top on in the hot sun during the first day or two of a holiday.

In Mediterranean countries particularly you should slurp on plenty of sunscreen cream with a relatively high protection factor (at least no. 5). These measures will not only help prevent your child from getting sunburn – but will also help protect him against skin cancer later on in life (since this so often is due to exposure to sunlight).

Treatment of sunburn in children is not very easy, and a badly sunburned child is (alas) in for some hours of pain, whatever you do. I'd recommend the following regime:

1   give the child paracetamol – it's often forgotten that this relieves sunburn pain too
2   apply calamine lotion
3   put him to bed in a cool room, with loose clothing and loose bedclothes, so that there's no rubbing on his skin.

Chemists sell stronger remedies, but these are highly controversial. They are:

anti-histamine creams. Many doctors are doubtful if these do any good, and dermatologists tend to be against them because there's a danger that they may sensitize the child's skin and cause a very painful reaction;

local anaesthetic creams and sprays. Preparations such as Solarcaine are dramatically effective in relieving sunburn pain. But (as I can testify from bitter personal experience) they can sometimes cause a really violent and painful sensitivity reaction – with the child's skin possibly remaining sensitive to local anaesthetics for life.

Sunstroke Symptoms include severe headache, weakness, irritability, thirst and even confusion. Astonishingly, this kind of reaction among small children can occur after just a few hours' exposure to the sun in England!

Treatment involves putting the youngster to bed in a darkened room, and giving him plenty of iced drinks. In the type of mild cases seen in Britain, he is usually better within forty-eight hours.

SYDENHAM'S CHOREA

See *St Vitus' dance*.

TB *(Tuberculosis)*

Tuberculosis is now rare in Britain, except among children of Asian origin. However, occasional outbreaks do occur when youngsters are in contact with an adult who is coughing up TB germs.

Most cases of tuberculosis occur in the lungs (pulmonary TB), but sometimes the bones and other organs are affected. A tubercular type of meningitis (see *Meningitis*) also occurs in children.

Fortunately, early treatment of most types of TB is successful in nearly all cases.

In practice, your child is very unlikely to catch TB if he follows the standard immunization schedule (see *Immunization*). However, at the time of writing, there's a proposal to drop the routine test and just offer it to selected children. But for the moment, all schoolchildren should normally be offered the Mantoux or Heaf test between the ages of ten and thirteen to see if they have any immunity to TB.

Most children don't have any immunity these days, so they are then given the protective BCG vaccine.

(In some areas, the risk of TB to Asian babies is considered sufficiently great for them to be given BCG soon after birth.)

TEMPER TANTRUMS

The two important things to remember about temper tantrums are:
- keep calm;
- you must *win*!

Again and again, I watch parents breaking either of these rules – and sometimes both. Let's look at them individually:

Keep calm An amazing number of parents respond to a temper tantrum by getting furious, by striking the child, and even by swearing at him. (The night before I wrote this, I watched a father do all these things to an upset child on a railway platform – naturally this just made everything worse.)

If you react to the child's tantrum by becoming all het up, he will realize that he's found a way of 'getting you going'. On the other hand, if you react coolly but firmly, he'll rapidly learn that tantrums don't seem to have much effect on you – and that therefore there's not a lot of point in having them!

You must win If you give in just *once* to a child's tantrum, you start him on a slippery slope. He soon learns that it's well worth while doing this kind of thing. He'll carry on shouting 'But I *want* that ice-cream!' (or whatever) for the rest of his life. If that's what you want, then by all means give in to him. . . .

See also *Hyperactivity*.

TEMPERATURE

If you have a child, you should have a thermometer in the house – because children so often get raised temperatures.

Taking a temperature is quite straightforward. Having bought a thermometer, have a look at the markings on it, which will be like the ones shown in the illustration on p. 131.

If you're very long-sighted, you might need a magnifying glass, but in practice nearly everyone can read the figures. The side of the thermometer forms a sort of lens, so that the column of mercury appears much wider than it really is, and so is easy to see.

Until recently, the figures on all British thermometers were in degrees fahrenheit (°F), which most people vaguely understood. You will now find it very difficult to buy a fahrenheit thermometer; they are now mostly marked in degrees centigrade (°C).

However, since there are still plenty of elderly fahrenheit thermometers floating around the homes of Britain, I'm going to try to explain both systems.

Your thermometer will be marked in degrees, reading from left to right. Fahrenheit thermometers read from about 94°F to about 107°F; centigrade from about 34°C to about 42°C. In between the degree marks, there are smaller lines which represent either fifths (0·2) or tenths (0·1) of a degree.

You'll see that at the 'normal' mark, there's an arrow, or the letter N, or both. On fahrenheit thermometers, this is at either 98·4 or 98·6. On centigrade instruments, it's at either 36·9 or 37.

If you're in the very common situation of being more or less familiar with the fahrenheit system, and only able to get hold of a centigrade thermometer, then this conversion table between the two scales will help you:

Degrees		
Fahrenheit	Centigrade	
95	35	Rather cold
96	35·6	
97	36·1	Of no
98	36·7	significance
99	37·2	
100	37·8	Fairly warm
101	38·3	
102	38·9	Hot – and
103	39·4	over the
104	40	'convulsion threshold' – see text
105	40·6	Very, very
106	41·1	hot – always contact doctor

Before using the thermometer, first make sure that the mercury column is down below the lower end of the scale. If it isn't, then shake it down – you do this by holding the upper end of the thermometer (the one at the other end from the bulb) and snapping the instrument sharply downwards four or five times with a firm, wristy action. This is tricky at first, but it soon comes with a little practice.

Having shaken the thermometer down, put it in the child's mouth, with the bulb under his tongue. (All tempera-tures quoted in this section and most others are mouth readings.)

Having seen one of my own toddlers bite the end off a thermometer and cheerfully spit the bits out, I can warn you that a child under about three can't be trusted to keep one of these things in his mouth without crunching it! So, in the case of younger children, you'll have to use the armpit – just hold the child's arm gently but firmly across his chest or tummy so that the bulb is kept warm under his arm.

Armpit temperatures are slightly lower than mouth ones – usually about 0·6°C or 1°F lower. But if you're telling the doctor your child's temperature over the telephone (which is often very helpful for him), don't add on a bit for this – it'll only cause confusion. Just tell him it's an armpit temperature.

I wouldn't advise you to try and take your child's temperature by putting the instrument up his bottom. He won't like it – and it can be dangerous.

Although many thermometers are marked 'Half Minute', always leave the instrument in the mouth or armpit for at least two minutes. At the end of that time, withdraw it and read it.

After reading it, shake it down, as before. Wash it in soap and water (cold water – hot water will blast the mercury through the roof) and then return it to its case.

If you're going to take your child's temperature again later that day, you could just stand the thermometer in a little jar of mild disinfectant until you need to use it again. This is a good hygienic practice if you've got more than one child ill in the family at the same time, since it helps prevent spread of infection.

As you'll see from the table above,

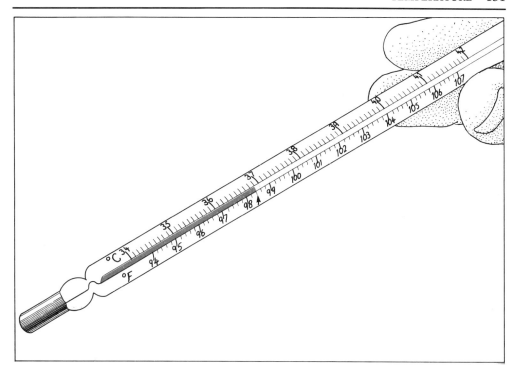

small variations from the normal body temperature are of no significance. No child's temperature stays fixed at normal – it moves up and down a bit during the course of the day, and the weather and the room temperature affect it. It'll go up if he runs about – and it'll also go up a bit if he's been crying a lot.

You don't have to worry about low temperatures, except in the unlikely event that your child is suffering from exposure. There are no common diseases of childhood which produce a low temperature.

However, if your baby has somehow or other been left in a cold room (or if an older child has been lost for hours in freezing cold weather) then take his temperature. If it's below 35·6°C (96°F), wrap him in plenty of blankets and inform your doctor.

How high a temperature means that something's wrong? If you look at the table, you'll see that 100–101°F or 37·8–38·3°C are really only considered 'fairly warm' in a child. Such temperatures can be associated with serious trouble – but plenty of children who only have a cold will have readings of this level.

But the next section of the table is from 38·9 to 40°C (that's 102 to 104°F). In this area, something definitely is wrong. Furthermore, a baby or toddler whose temperature gets up to this level runs at least some risk of having a convulsion – simply because of the effect of the high temperature on his immature brain. (See *Feverish convulsions*)

Finally, if your child is in the last section of the table – 40·6°C (105°F) or over – then something is *very* wrong and you must contact a doctor at once.

Apart from temperatures brought on

by crying or running around, a high temperature is almost always due to some sort of infection, for instance: colds and other virus infections; 'flu; tonsillitis; ear infection (otitis media); chest infection (including bronchitis and pneumonia); kidney infection (pyelitis); gastroenteritis; mumps; measles; chickenpox; German measles; whooping cough; meningitis. See under the relevant headings.

Appendicitis can also cause a moderately raised temperature. And excessive exposure to sunshine – common even on the holiday beaches of Britain – is a frequent cause of a raised temperature and a headache. See *Appendicitis* and *Sunburn*.

TETANUS

See *Lockjaw*.

THRUSH

Thrush is an infection which affects both young babies and adult women (especially pregnant women).

It's caused by a fungus, and you may also hear it referred to as candida or monilia.

Thrush attacks the baby in the mouth, and gives her little sore patches inside her cheeks and on her tongue, which may make her cry a lot. Characteristically, there are quite large white blobs of fungus material on the tongue and inside the cheeks and this appearance helps the doctor to make the diagnosis. She will almost certainly prescribe nystatin drops to be instilled into the baby's

mouth, which should clear it up very quickly, and the odds are that the trouble will not recur.

You may wonder where the baby got the thrush from, and the answer is that while one can't say for certain (since so many people are carriers of thrush), there is always quite a chance that it has come from the mother's vagina during delivery. So if the mother of a baby with thrush has had any soreness in that area, she should get it treated by her doctor. (Her husband may need treatment too with an anti-fungus cream.) The doctor may well also give general hygiene advice about avoiding tights and hot baths – both of which tend to encourage growth of thrush in the vagina.

TICS

These are habitual sudden jerky movements.

Often a child develops a tic because he's worried or disturbed about something. This is not his fault, and there is no point whatever in punishing him because of the tic – or even in drawing attention to it.

What you need to do is to find out why he's uneasy in his mind – and take appropriate action to relieve his anxiety. If a tic is really bad, you may need the help of a psychologist. Begin by consulting your GP, or (if it seems that school problems are looming large in your child's mind) ask the head teacher about seeing the school's educational psychologist.

Sometimes tics are associated with cerebral palsy (see *Spastic disorders*). See also *Stress in childhood*.

TOADSTOOL POISONING

See *Fungus poisoning*.

TOENAIL, INGROWING

See *Ingrowing toenail*.

TONSILLITIS AND

TONSILLECTOMY

Tonsillitis is one of the most common illnesses of children, yet many parents know next to nothing about it. Rather surprisingly, many family health books don't even describe the symptoms correctly!

Tonsillitis just means inflammation of the tonsils – and it's caused by infection. The tonsils are little blobs of tissue situated at the back of the throat, one on either side. If you look in a child's mouth, you'll see them hanging down like a pair of rather baggy pink curtains – and leaving a remarkably small hole for both the food and breath to get through!

The function of these two swellings is protective. In other words, they're full of cells that help to mop up germs that enter the body via the mouth. They form a sort of guardian ring around the top of the child's airway.

When they are small, children are subjected to an enormous barrage of germs. Especially when they first go to school (or playschool), millions upon millions of germs of types which they've never encountered before come drifting into their mouths. Many of these micro-organisms would, if unchecked, be only too delighted to set up some really unpleasant infection, like pneumonia or severe bronchitis.

Fortunately, for the child, the tonsils are there to trap a lot of these germs. The cells inside the tonsils gobble up most of the germs and soon render them completely harmless.

But (and it's a very big but) trouble comes when, as so very often happens, the tonsils are overwhelmed. When that happens, they become big, red, inflamed and sometimes covered in pus.

The term tonsillitis covers anything from a very mild inflammation to a really roaring one.

Mild tonsillitis   Happily, most of the time the inflammation is mild. If you looked at the child's tonsils, you'd see that they were a bit red and a bit enlarged. But, of course, as you probably don't go around peering down your child's throat, you never know that his tonsils are slightly inflamed.

Indeed, all you may notice is that he's a bit off-colour, and a bit grumpy. He may be off his food too, and have a very slight cough. You may decide to keep him off school for the day or give him a little paracetamol. By the morning, he's obviously well on the road to recovery, and that's that – you forget all about the episode, and so does he! No one ever realizes that he's had a very mild bout of what is, technically speaking, mild tonsillitis.

But if his symptoms are a bit worse than this and you decide to take him to your GP, don't panic if the doctor mentions the phrase 'mild tonsillitis'. This doesn't mean that his tonsils have to be removed. Mild tonsillitis in children is simply the equivalent of an adult's sore throat. For some odd reason, very young children don't often complain of actual pain in the throat – but otherwise there is virtually no difference between the two conditions.

Severe tonsillitis   If you've got a child who's had a bad bout of tonsillitis, you'll know about it. She will feel absolutely rotten. She's completely off her food, and if anybody tries to give her any she vomits. This is in fact a rather little-known hallmark of severe tonsillitis. Anything and everything you try to give the youngster is puked violently back at you! She also has a bit of a cough, swollen glands at the side of the neck, and a temperature. Her tummy may ache a bit because the stomach ('mesenteric') glands have come out in sympathy.

This kind of tonsillitis does need medical advice. Whether you ask the doctor to call or take the youngster down to the surgery to be examined is sometimes difficult to decide: if in doubt, ring your doctor and ask.

Treatment is obviously up to the individual doctor. A family doctor often has no immediate way of telling the difference between an infection caused by viruses and one caused by bacteria. So if the child is really poorly he will almost always prescribe an antibiotic in the hope that the infection is a bacterial one. (He may take a throat swab, which can help to indicate a bacterial infection, but the result won't be available to him for several days.)

The practice of hospital doctors tends to be rather different: if a child is in the (fairly uncommon) situation of being treated for tonsillitis in hospital, the paediatrician will probably just give him paracetamol and plenty of fluids, and keep him under the sort of close observation which is possible in a hospital ward. Very often the child will get better in a matter of hours without the need for antibiotics. However, this sort of close-observation medicine is rather difficult in general practice, which is why most GPs feel it is safer simply to give antibiotics.

The antibiotics are usually given in a pleasantly flavoured syrup – some at least of which should stay down even if the child is vomiting a lot. Only if retching is very severe will a doctor put a child through the ordeal of having to have antibiotics by injection.

Otherwise the mainstays of treatment of severe tonsillitis are:

- give plenty of fluids (preferably iced)
- don't attempt to give food
- give a little paracetamol in accordance with the doctor's instructions
- try to keep the child's temperature down – *don't* overheat him (see *Feverish convulsions*).

Most children with even the severest bout of tonsillitis will be better in a few days or so. Some may never have another really bad bout, but others will have an occasional one – or perhaps even two or three a year.

Tonsillectomy   This means removal of the tonsils. Well over 100,000 British children still have this done each year – which is far too many, especially as the operation is very often done for little or no reason.

Admittedly, some children do benefit but many others *don't*, and have gone through a trying and traumatic procedure for nothing. Also, the operation does carry a very small but measurable risk of death.

I'd advise you not to have the operation done unless both your GP and a paediatrician feel it's necessary. (Paediatricians tend to be less in favour of tonsillectomy than surgeons.)

The operation is practically always done under general anaesthetic these days, and the surgeon works through the child's mouth, cutting the tonsils away from the throat wall.

The operation takes only a few minutes, but it'll be a week or two before the child recovers fully. During that time, he will have a very sore throat indeed. He'll need lots of soothing gargles (hot salt water is good), probably some paracetamol – and lots of love!

TOOTHACHE

Children should never get toothache – because toothache is caused by tooth decay, which really shouldn't occur today.

If you insist that your children clean their teeth thoroughly, two or three times a day; if you take them to the dentist twice a year; and if you reach a joint decision with him about whether you want them to have fluoride 'painting' or use fluoride tablets – then the risk of toothache occurring becomes very small indeed.

But if it happens, soak a bit of cotton wool in oil of cloves, and place on the affected tooth. All you can do is give her paracetamol, and try and get an urgent appointment with the dentist.

This may be difficult (especially at a weekend), but if you can't reach your dentist or if he's not willing to see you, remember that your family isn't signed up with a family dentist in the same way that they're signed up with a family GP.

So it's worth picking up the Yellow Pages and ringing around to try and find a dentist who will see your child.

If you live anywhere near a teaching hospital try calling their dental department – which *may* provide an emergency out-of-hours service.

TRAVEL SICKNESS

Car sickness is very common, very trying – and very messy!

It's probably caused by a combination of things: the bumping up and down of the car; the slight disorientation which some children feel when looking at scenery whipping past through a rear window; excitement; and the fear of sickness itself.

Good moves are as follows:

1 Don't suggest to the child that he'll probably be ill
2 Give him lots of games to occupy his mind
3 On long journeys, it's certainly worth giving a sickness-prone child an anti-sickness pill – at least an hour before you leave
4 Avoid big meals before and during the journey
5 Make sure you have plenty of large, stout bags.

There's no evidence that static electricity causes car sickness, but if you want to fit one of those little earth conductors to your car, it'll do no harm. Make sure you tell the youngster what you're doing, because the power of suggestion may influence him considerably!

Most of what I've said about car sickness applies to air and seasickness, too. When flying, the necessary bags are thoughtfully provided! Unfortunately, you may find that if the weather is bad at sea nothing will work . . . (You could always try leading the family in a chorus of 'Abide with Me'.)

TUMMY ACHE

See *Abdominal pain.*

TYPHOID FEVER

This bowel infection is now very rare in Britain – but can be caught in Mediterranean holiday countries.

Chief symptoms include fever, malaise, abdominal discomfort and constipation or diarrhoea.

So see your doctor well before going abroad and discuss whether your child (and you) should have the typhoid jab – which (unfortunately) often produces a rather painful reaction. See also *Immunization.*

ULCERATIVE COLITIS

This is a disease – quite common in adults, but fortunately quite rare in children – in which the colon (large bowel) keeps becoming inflamed. Its cause is unknown – though a few doctors have suggested that sensitivity to cow's milk might play a part. The symptoms are recurrent severe diarrhoea; abdominal pain and discomfort; bleeding from the bowel; weakness and weight loss.

Ulcerative colitis is therefore a pretty trying and distressing disorder for a child. Fortunately, symptoms can very often be controlled by the use of steroids

(cortisone-like drugs), though these can have major side-effects. Steroids are often given by enema.

Other therapies include the use of a helpful drug called sulphasalazine (Salazopyrin), plus the administration of vitamins and iron.

Regrettably, in a few cases it's necessary to remove the child's entire colon. This is a major operation, but may sometimes be life-saving.

UNCONSCIOUSNESS

This can have many causes, including fits (see *Epilepsy;* also *Feverish convulsions*) and simple faints (see *Fainting*).

For treatment, see *Unconsciousness,* under *First Aid.*

URINARY PROBLEMS

There are several urinary problems which are liable to occur in childhood: bed-wetting (see: *Bed-wetting*); urinary blockage due to tightness of the foreskin (see: *Circumcision*); and urinary infections.

Infections in the waterworks are moderately common in little girls, but rare in little boys. This is mainly because male children have a much longer urinary pipe (urethra), with its opening far further away from that rich source of germs, the anus.

So to prevent bowel germs from getting from the anus to the urinary opening (and so causing infection), all little girls should be encouraged to wipe their bottoms *backwards*, rather than forwards.

Chief symptoms of urinary infection are: pain passing water; frequency of passing water; and possibly blood in the wee. If the urinary infection climbs up to the kidneys, there may be pain in the small of the back, a raised temperature and uncontrollable shivering.

Always take your child to the doctor if she has symptoms suggesting urinary infection. The doctor should send a specimen of her urine to the hospital path. lab. – and may well want to do x-rays of the child's urinary passages. The usual treatment is a full course of antibiotics – but further measures may be necessary, depending on the results of the tests.

URTICARIA

Often known as hives or nettle rash, this is a common skin reaction which does actually look very like the white lumpy appearance which most people get when they're stung by nettles. But in urticaria, there are usually quite large raised, white, puffy areas of skin – as opposed to the fairly small spots caused by a nettle sting.

Some children seem to be particularly liable to develop urticaria, often because their skins are very sensitive to chemicals (including tartrazine – the yellow food dye known as E102); drugs (including penicillin and aspirin) and certain foodstuffs.

Other youngsters develop it when they're exposed to sunlight, or to cold. In a minority of cases, it's a reaction to the presence of worms (see *Worms*).

Happily, most minor bouts of urticaria will go away on their own. In a very severe attack, it might be necessary for your doctor to give injections of steroids, antihistamines or adrenalin. Antihistamine tablets may also be helpful. Naturally, in recurrent urticaria, you should try and find out what's causing the attacks – and make sure the child avoids it.

Papular urticaria is a condition characterized by little lumps about one to five millimetres across. Its cause used to be a mystery – but it's now known to be simply due to insect bites, for instance by midges.

VACCINATION

See *Immunization*.

VERRUCA

Although people sometimes tend to get a bit panicky about the word verruca, it's just a wart on the foot, caused by a virus. Vast numbers of children develop verrucas each year.

They are mildly infectious, so your child should not swan around barefoot in changing rooms and swimming baths till she's cured. If you buy one of those little verruca socks (from a sports shop), she'll be able to wear it at the pool and so not miss swimming.

It is easy to get a bit fed up when treatment of verrucas doesn't seem to be working. My own experience is that the standard applications which family doctors tend to prescribe for you to apply *yourself* do take ages to take effect – and sometimes fail altogether.

An alternative is to go to a good chiropodist, who will probably burn the verruca away with a (painless) acid application.

Some family doctors and dermatologists use cold probes (cryotherapy) to burn the verruca away. And some surgeons (and, indeed, some casualty departments) use curetting – that is, scooping the verruca out with a spoon-like cutting instrument. This is, however, a bit of a bloody business, which in my experience frightens lots of kids. In short, my advice is to go to a chiropodist if you can afford it.

VERTIGO

See *Giddiness*.

VITAMIN DEFICIENCY

Vitamin deficiency is incredibly rare in British children. For example, I have not myself seen a single case of vitamin deficiency in the last twenty-five years.

There are certain very uncommon vitamin-deficiency diseases which do occur every now and again, and they're listed in this book under their own individual headings (see *Rickets*; *Scurvy*). In practice, the only one which is likely to occur in Britain is rickets in Asian children.

None the less, many parents do give their school-age kids regular vitamin supplements. Not long ago, one of my son's teachers asked his class to raise their hands if their parents were giving them vitamins. Every single boy raised his arm – except for the ones who were the sons of doctors!

Anyway, if you do want to give your child regular vitamins, you're most unlikely to do him any harm by doing so (though there's not much chance you'll do him any good, either).

However, the situation is rather different with small babies. Breast-fed babies will get enough vitamins from their mother's milk. Bottle-fed babies will probably *not* get enough vitamin C and D if they are just fed on cow's milk (which – surprisingly enough – is still used by some mothers). Commercial dried milks do contain added vitamins. Doctors and health visitors vary wildly in the advice they give to mothers about vitamin supplements – but many do suggest that if the baby is bottle-fed, he should be given vitamin drops such as Abidec, which contains vitamins A, B, C and D. Others think that it's enough just to give the child orange juice or tomato juice (no Worcester sauce, please!).

But once a child is weaned on to a mixed diet with milk, fruit and vegetables, there's really no point in going on with vitamin drops.

If you do use drops (or fish liver oils), please do not exceed the stated dose, as this can be dangerous.

VOMITING

After years of both parenthood and paediatrics, I'd like to pass on this valuable tip. If a child says she may vomit, believe her! Grab a large bowl or a stout plastic bag and (if possible) head for the nearest loo. Following my own advice has saved me many a clearing-up job over the years.

Now here are the common causes of vomiting in children:

• tummy infections caused by germs.

These frequently (though not always) cause diarrhoea as well. (See *Diarrhoea*.) Vomiting in a young baby can rapidly cause dangerous dehydration. So repeated vomiting in a baby always demands medical advice.

- tonsillitis (see: *Tonsillitis*). Most parents (and most family medical guides) seem to be unaware that when a child feels off colour and vomits, the reason is often an infection of the tonsils – probably because the enlarged tonsils press against the back of his throat and make him gag.

Rather less common causes of vomiting include:

- scarlet fever (see *Scarlet Fever*)
- pneumonia (see *Pneumonia*)
- severe catarrh dripping down the back of the throat
- whooping cough (see *Whooping Cough*),
- psychological or hysterical vomiting;
- deliberate (i.e. self-induced) vomiting – e.g. to avoid school.
- appendicitis – though the child with an acute appendix rarely vomits more than once or twice (see *Appendicitis*);
- migraine (see *Migraine*).

Rare causes of vomiting include:

- pyloric stenosis
- meningitis
- Reye's syndrome
- poisoning
- over-eating.

For what to do in each of these cases, see the advice under individual entries.

WARTS

Warts are small benign growths on a child's skin, caused by a virus. They're mildly infectious and children seem to be most vulnerable to them at playschool and in their early schoolday years. After that, they mostly seem to develop a resistance.

Medical treatment of warts is still not very satisfactory – which is why people still claim that after the doctor failed them, they got better results with some sort of traditional wart-charming remedy.

In practice, most childhood warts (not all) do just drop off after a few months – which is why almost anything you do to them can appear to produce a cure.

Treatment for warts is very much the same as for verrucas (see *Verrucas*). Your GP might suggest application of a gel or acid solution to try and get rid of the wart; burning it out with a hot cautery; freezing it; or cutting it out with a surgical instrument.

Although warts are slightly infectious, there's not really a lot of point in covering them unless the child is embarrassed about them, or he keeps knocking them on things.

WASP STINGS

See *Stings*, under *First Aid*.

WAX

Some children get a lot of wax in their ears, others don't. This seems to be genetically determined.

It doesn't matter if your child's ear glands make a lot of wax. All you need do is keep an eye out for the symptom that wax has been building up again –

namely deafness (specially after swimming).

When this happens, take the youngster to the doctor, who will tell you if her ears need syringing. This takes about five minutes, and shouldn't be painful – though the child may find it a bit alarming, especially if no one's had the sense to explain to her beforehand what the doctor or nurse is going to do.

The doctor can also advise you about whether in the future it might be advisable to use wax-dissolving drops (e.g. Cerumol) to prevent build-up of wax.

Don't try and keep the wax at bay by digging around in your child's ears – and don't let her poke things in either. This could damage the eardrum and may cause infection.

WHEEZINESS

Wheeziness in a child's chest is pretty well always caused by narrowing of the air tubes and/or mucus in the air tubes.

This symptom suggests the possible presence of asthma (see *Asthma*) or asthmatic bronchitis (see *Bronchitis*). So if your child wheezes, you should definitely have his chest 'sounded' by your doctor.

WHITLOW *(Paronychia)*

This annoying little infection often produces redness, swelling and pain right next to the child's fingernail or toenail.

The germs may have got in through a hang-nail or crack in the skin – or as a result of an ingrowing toenail (see *Ingrowing toenail*).

Most doctors will treat a child's whitlow with antibiotics. But if there's obviously pus present, then the whitlow will have to be lanced (opened).

WHOOPING COUGH

This fairly common disease of childhood causes a great deal of distress to both child and parent, and also causes a few deaths, mainly among young babies.

Your child can be immunized against whooping cough (there is great controversy about this at present), but first, about the infection itself. Whooping cough is caused by a germ called Bordetella pertussis. (Pertussis is the posh name for whooping cough.)

This germ, like so many others, is acquired through breathing it in. If a child who's got whooping cough (or who's just developing it) breathes or coughs or sneezes in the general direction of your child, then there's a high chance that he will catch it, unless he's immunized – and even that doesn't give him complete protection.

About twelve days later, your child may well get what seems at first to be just a bit of a cold and cough. Unfortunately, it's almost impossible to make a diagnosis of whooping cough at this early stage – which is a pity, because your youngster is now highly infectious.

Probably the first suspicion you'll have that anything's wrong will be a week or so later when you realize that his cough just seems to be going on and on.

Very typically, the poor kid is racked by the most violent bouts of coughing which really distress him. He ends up each bout feeling and looking half-choked – and he may even be sick.

In many cases – but by no means all – there's the give-away symptom of a whoop. This is a crowing noise caused by the child's sudden desperate intake of breath at the end of the bout of coughing. Once you've heard that, then you know he's got whooping cough.

Regrettably, the coughing and choking and whooping may go on for at least two weeks – and sometimes much more. (My own eldest went on coughing and spluttering as though her heart would break for about five weeks – and she'd been vaccinated, so the infection was milder in her than in an unvaccinated child.)

So all in all, the illness isn't much fun for the child, or the parents. Be prepared to sit up on many nights, consoling and cuddling your child, and to spend quite a bit of time cleaning puke off the sheets!

The greatest danger is to young babies, and they usually have to be admitted to hospital. But toddlers and schoolchildren are usually nursed at home. Your doctor will come and see the child and if he agrees that it's whooping cough he'll probably prescribe a course of the antibiotic erythromycin.

Although this doesn't affect the child's symptoms (except just possibly if it's given very early in the illness), it will make him non-infectious within a few days – a matter of great importance, especially if there's a baby in the house.

In fact, there is no cure for whooping cough. So all that can be done is to make the child as comfortable and as happy as possible, under what are bound to be difficult circumstances.

Your doctor will prescribe whatever medication he thinks will relieve the youngster's symptoms a bit. GPs often give anti-vomiting drugs to try to prevent the distressing retching that frequently follows each bout of coughing. They may also prescribe inhalations and cough medicine – though there's some argument about whether the cough medicine is really of any value, except for its sedative effect.

When my own daughter had whooping cough, we found that putting her in a moist atmosphere was very helpful – for instance, sitting her in a steaming bath. Taking her out in the fresh air for a gentle stroll also helped. Paroxysms were worst at night, and the best thing seemed to be to sit her up and cuddle her until she dropped off to sleep.

Meals, incidentally, should be small and light. The child will have the best chance of keeping them down if you give them soon after a coughing/vomiting attack.

Do have a potty or some other container – plus a towel – by the side of the bed all the time until the youngster's feeling a bit better. Otherwise, you really will have puke everywhere.

When the youngster seems very bunged up with mucus in the throat and chest, it may be helpful to go in for a little bit of do-it-yourself physiotherapy. Get him to lie on his front with his head and arms hanging over the edge of the bed. Then gently slap the back and sides of his chest to help shift the secretions, and encourage him to cough them up. (By the way, don't do this while he's in one of the coughing/whooping bouts – this simple exercise is to be done during one of the quiet periods in between fits of coughing.)

Possible complications of whooping

cough include pneumonia, lung damage, ear trouble and convulsions. The death rate in recent years has been relatively low – about one in every 5000 cases – but is higher in the very young.

However, the incidence of lung trouble is so high that some doctors think that every child who has had whooping cough should have an x-ray afterwards to ensure that all is well.

So, should your children have the whooping cough jab?

As I've said above, there have been very alarming reports in recent years about the vaccine causing brain damage to tiny tots. What is the risk of this?

Unfortunately, it's very hard to assess. Frankly, the health authorities don't know what the chances are of a child developing brain damage as a result of being given the whooping cough immunization. They claim that the risks are very low indeed – and a few doctors have even gone so far as to express doubt as to whether the jab can cause brain damage at all.

But parents who claim that their children have been made mentally subnormal by the injection think that the authorities are playing the risks down. They maintain that there is really quite an appreciable danger that the vaccine may harm a child's brain.

However, let's not forget the other side of the coin. As I hope I've made clear above, whooping cough can be a very serious disease – and it can even kill.

Admittedly, quite a lot of deaths occur in babies who are still too young to be immunized (for technical reasons, you can't start a course of immunization till a child is about three months old). For this reason, opponents of the vaccine claim that it isn't all that useful:

they say that by the time doctors give it to babies, they're already past the age when whooping cough poses the greatest threat to life.

Against that, you have to bear in mind that by immunizing children against whooping cough on a national scale, we are preventing epidemics of the disease – and thereby indirectly protecting the young babies who are still too small to be vaccinated.

It's going to be some years before the arguments for and against whooping cough vaccination are settled. In the meantime, what should you do, as a parent?

For what it's worth, my advice is this. Because the decision as to whether to have the jab or not is such a difficult one, you should go to your GP and/or child health clinic and talk it over very carefully indeed before making up your mind. Don't let anybody rush you into anything, and don't come to any hurried decisions.

Ask your GP or the clinic doctor what the risks of getting whooping cough are in your area of the country. In general, the risk of catching it is greater in towns, and where there is overcrowding, than it is in the country. Tell the doctor if you're living in crowded accommodation – and tell him if there are any other children in the household.

Also, ask him if there are any special reasons why your youngster shouldn't have the jab. Common contra-indications of this sort include:

- A history of fits;
- An odd reaction to a previous whooping cough jab (there are three jabs in the course);
- A difficult birth, during which your child's brain was short of oxygen.

Some doctors are doubtful about giving the jab where there is a strong family history of fits. But I think I should make clear that a recent opinion poll of GPs, which I helped to arrange for *General Practitioner*, showed that the majority of British family doctors are still very much in favour of the injection – presumably because they're well aware of what an unpleasant and downright dangerous illness whooping cough can be.

So the decision as to whether your child has the immunization or not is an individual one which *you* must make, with the help of your doctor or the infant welfare clinic doctor.

Several new vaccines (including a Japanese one) are on trial, and it's hoped that one of these will be safer.

There is also a controversial and much-publicized *homoeopathic* remedy which is described as a 'vaccine'. In fact it's not really a vaccine at all, and I don't think it'd be reasonable to regard it as an alternative way of protecting your child against whooping cough.

WIND

See *Colic.*

WORMS

Naturally, parents tend to get very alarmed about the idea of their child having worms! ('How could such a thing happen?' they cry. And the answer is: 'Very easily!')

Now there's nothing to be ashamed of in having worms. It happens in the best-regulated households, and the only thing to do is to get the child treated as fast as possible – and not to make a big fuss about it, or make her feel upset.

In some cases, the doctor will want to treat the whole family – including Mum and Dad. This arouses considerable indignation in some parents! But it's best to comply – otherwise the worms may keep going round and round the family.

Puppies and kittens very frequently have worms. The risk to your child is, surprisingly enough, not all that great. But you should have any dog or cat de-wormed by your vet as a matter of routine. And you should not let your child play in areas that may be contamined with pet faeces.

There are four main types of worm which occur in Britain, but only one of them is really common. Rather surprisingly (and contrary to what many people believe) worms are most unlikely to be a cause of abdominal pain.

Threadworms These are the common ones. The symptom which they produce is night-time itching round the child's anus. The itching is caused by the female threadworm emerging from his bottom to lay her eggs. This makes him scratch his backside – and the eggs get under his fingernails.

From there, the eggs are easily transferred to his mouth – or to the mouths of other members of the family, or indeed friends.

You may be able to see the worms, looking like little white threads. Your doctor will probably want to treat the whole family with piperazine. In addition, cut the youngster's nails short – and make sure he washes his hands before meals.

Roundworms These look like white earthworms. Understandably, children are very alarmed at finding they've passed one of these with a bowel motion! Take the child (and the worm – for identification) to the doctor, and she will probably prescribe piperazine, and give advice about better toilet hygiene. This is important, because roundworm eggs are spread when faecal material contaminates food.

A different type of roundworm (*Toxocara canis*) has received a lot of publicity in recent years, because it is caught from puppies and may cause childhood blindness. In fact, blindness from this cause is very rare, but if you buy a puppy, you should take the common-sense precautions outlined above.

Hookworms These are almost entirely confined to Asian children – particularly those who have spent some time in the tropics. The infection is caught by walking in bare feet on ground which has been contaminated with human bowel motions containing hookworm larvae. The worm may cause anaemia, a cough and many other symptoms. Fortunately, drugs such as Alcopar are very effective.

Tapeworms These are ribbon-shaped worms which your child could only acquire through eating raw or badly-undercooked beef or pork. Not surprisingly, tapeworms are now very rare in the UK – since there are few toddlers who go for steak tartare! Niclosamide is an effective drug.

WRY NECK *(Torticollis)*

This is a curious symptom in which the child's head is twisted to one side. She may simply wake up with it and yell for help!

The cause is a spasm of the large muscle at the side of the neck (the sterno-mastoid) – but why this spasm should happen is unknown. Some cases are associated with a bout of tonsillitis (see *Tonsillitis*).

As a rule, there's no point in giving any treatment – apart from a couple of days in bed and a spot of warmth from a hotty applied to the neck. In most kids, wry neck will get better spontaneously (but pain-killing tablets might be necessary for a day or two).

If the condition hasn't cleared up within a week, it'd be worth considering having your child's neck manipulated by an osteopath or chiropractor. Alternatively, a few GPs use a relaxant drug called Robaxin Injectable, but this is quite powerful, and may cause dizziness.

A totally different form of wry neck sometimes occurs in newborn babies. It's caused by a swelling in the same muscle, and should clear up completely. Gentle rotation of the child's head from side to side is believed to help. You may hear the doctors inadvisedly call it a 'sterno-mastoid *tumour*' – but pay no attention, because it's *not* a malignant condition, and this unfortunate word 'tumour' just means 'swelling'.

Index